Small Business

S0-AUA-376

Small Business

Financial Planning for the Owner of the Business

Stoddart

Copyright © 1998 by Investors Group Inc.

Copyright © 1998 by Alpha Media™

All rights reserved. No part of this publication may be reproduced or transmitted in any form or by any means, electronic or mechanical, including photocopying, recording, or any information storage and retrieval system, without permission in writing from the publisher.

Published in 1998 by Stoddart Publishing Co. Limited
34 Lesmill Road, Toronto, Canada M3B 2T6
Toll-free tel. for Ontario & Quebec: 1-800-387-0141
Toll-free tel. for all other provinces & territories: 1-800-287-0172
Fax: (416) 445-5967   Email: customer.service@ccmailgw.genpub.com

Stoddart Books are available for bulk purchase for sales promotions, premiums, fundraising, and seminars. For details, contact the **Special Sales Department** at the above address.

Produced for Investors Group by Alpha Media™
151 Bloor St. W., Suite 890, Toronto, Canada M5S 1S4

02 01 00 99 98 1 2 3 4 5

Canadian Cataloguing in Publication Data

Main entry under title:

Small business: financial planning for the owner & the business

(The Investors Group series)
ISBN 0-896391-16-8

1. Businesspeople — Finance, Personal.   2. Small business — Finance.
I. Investors Group.   II. Series

HG179.S52 1998   332.024'338   C97-932566-8

JACKET AND TEXT DESIGN: Adele Webster/ArtPlus Limited
COVER ILLUSTRATION: Riccardo Stampatori
PAGE MAKE-UP: Heather Brunton/ArtPlus Limited

Printed and bound in Canada

The information contained in this publication is presented as a general source of information only and is not intended as a solicitation or recommendation to buy or sell specific investments, nor is it intended to provide legal advice. Prospective investors should review the annual report, simplified prospectus, and annual information form of a fund carefully before making an investment decision. No representations are made as to the accuracy of the information contained herein, and individuals should consult their professional advisor for advice based on their specific circumstances.

The INVESTORS GROUP word mark and IG design are registered trademarks owned by Investors Group Inc. and used under licence.

About Investors Group

Investors Group is a Canadian leader in providing personal financial services through financial planning, a unique family of mutual funds, and a comprehensive range of other investment products and services including retirement savings plans, insurance, mortgages and GICs.

The Investors Group story began in 1940, and we have grown to serve close to one million clients from coast to coast through a dedicated and professional sales force. At the heart of our efforts is a simple, long-term strategy — to work closely with clients to understand their current circumstances and investment preferences and help them achieve their long-term personal and financial goals.

Investors Group is a member of the Power Financial Corporation group of companies.

Acknowledgments

This book was the result of a collaboration among people at three companies. Susan Yates and Arnold Gosewich at Alpha Media initiated and co-ordinated the project. At Investors Group, a large and dedicated team of Chartered Financial Planners, accountants, lawyers, and investment specialists provided tax and financial planning information, as well as general direction on appropriate strategies for consumers in each life stage. At Colborne Communications Centre, Greg Ioannou, Sasha Chapman, and Peggy Ferguson co-ordinated the writing, editing, and indexing.

About This Book

Small Business is aimed at helping you, as a business owner, to manage your personal finances. The book focuses entirely on personal finance, not on the finances of your business. It will equip you to think more clearly and usefully about your own situation and will arm you with questions you can ask to help you reach your dreams. This book is not written as a "do it yourself" guide. In fact, many of the subjects discussed involve complex legal, financial, and tax issues that have been simplified to make them more approachable.

Because the details of each life and each business are different, it would be impossible to cover all of life's possibilities in one place. Readers are urged to seek professional advice on their personal circumstances.

About This Series

Small Business, designed to address the special investment needs of the small business owner, is the fourth book in a four-part series. The other three books are:

Starting Out, for beginning investors;

Prime Time, for intermediate investors, and especially those who are interested in retirement planning; and

Retire Ready, for investors who have already retired.

Contents

CHAPTER 1

Financial Freedom for the Small Business Owner

You, Your Business, and Your Future

Freedom. Opportunity. Dreams. That's what financial planning is all about. No matter who you are, what kind of business you own, or how old you are, you have dreams you want to realize. But what your personal future holds will affect your business, and vice versa, and your challenge is going to be to learn how to balance these two intertwined parts of your life. Striking that balance by learning how to manage your money will make your dreams and hopes for the future a reality. You want your business to continue to grow — maybe you'll branch out, go international, and hire new employees. You might also want to buy a new house. Maybe a vacation property. That's the domain of wise financial planning. What about the future? Will you retire? Slow down? What will happen to your business? Will you wind it down as you wind down? Will you pass it on to someone? Do you want to see your children continue in the business? Or will it close its doors the day you die? Whether your family has one or two incomes, whether your business is starting, growing, or expanding, you can make your money go further by managing it better.

The Big Secret

Personal finance is not a cold-blooded, penny-pinching exercise in dollar signs and decimal points. In fact, it's a warm and human activity, because it's all about turning potential into reality. Managing your money allows you to get more bang for every buck — and that means achieving your goals and living the life you want to live. The fact that you're reading this book shows that you want to make the best possible life for yourself, and keep your business interests in mind, too. Everyone deserves personal and family financial independence and has the ability to achieve it. Add common sense, awareness of your key goals, and a willingness to strengthen some of your financial habits, and you're on your way.

Good and Not-So-Good Times

Owning your own business means being totally self-reliant. Self-reliance has never been more important when it comes to personal finance, and everything tells us that we're going to have to depend on ourselves more and on others less. As a small business owner, you have part of the problem licked: you take your own risks, make your own decisions. You are in charge. Unlike an employee of a corporation, you don't have to worry about downsizing and outsourcing, but the financial stability of your business is a major concern. But as with every citizen, government decisions about our social safety net make it even more important for you to take care of your own future. In general, it's harder to qualify for benefits, the benefits are often smaller than they were in the past, and you have to make larger contributions. This makes planning for your retirement more important

WHAT EXACTLY IS FINANCIAL PLANNING ANYWAY?

Financial planning is:

- preparing for retirement;
- minimizing tax;
- using debt and credit effectively;
- preparing for unexpected financial obligations;
- protecting yourself and your family against loss of income, either through death or disability; and
- being able to earn better returns from your investments, with acceptable risk.

Financial planning essentially means paying attention to the money you have today and planning for your future.

than ever. And because Canadians are living longer, you not only have to look after yourself better, you'll have to do it for a longer time. So financial planning really is for you. Especially as a small business owner, since the flip side of independence is that you have only yourself to fall back on. Take charge of your money, and it will cushion the bad times and make the good ones better. It will help you get where you want to go in comfort.

Cheques and Balances

As a business owner, you are in a unique position. You don't go to work each day and collect a paycheque from an employer. Rather, you are your own boss, and often you have a staff and a payroll to deal with yourself. But like the corporate employee, you also have a home life and private financial responsibilities. You are faced with the challenge of keeping these two parts of your life in balance. If you are incorporated, the law may prevent creditors from making claims on your non-business assets in the event of business bankruptcy, but no one can prevent you from straining your personal finances to buttress your business. The key to small business sanity is establishing and maintaining a balance between these two parts of your life.

Taking Charge of Your Financial Life

Your financial plan will be as individual as your fingerprints because it has to fit you — your goals and your circumstances. But the basic components are common to all successful financial approaches, and they are reassuringly simple. The key is to identify the major lifestyle goals, set financial goals to match, and then work out financial strategies that will get you there. So start with information and then apply it.

- Identify your most important short-term goals, those that apply over the next five years. Then set out your longer-term ones, say for the next 10 or 20 years. List them in order of importance.
- Organize. You're probably an old hand at it, but are your personal finances as organized as your business finances? The ability to assess your current situation depends on your ability to keep it all straight. If you haven't, invest some time now in clearing out those drawers of paper at home.

FIVE STEPS TOWARDS FINANCIAL INDEPENDENCE

1. Plan your long-term goals:
   - Know where you want to be in 10 years (i.e., which large lump-sum purchases you'd like to make, such as a truck, a house, or a vacation property), and start saving for those goals.
   - Invest in RRSPs. Retirement is closer than you think.
   - Start a regular savings program to ensure that post-secondary education is affordable for your children.
   - Know how you want your business to evolve in the future, and think about how you want to sell, pass on, or wind down the business.
2. Manage your debt and expenses:
   - Get your cash flow under control.
   - Use debt wisely and pay off your highest-cost non-tax-deductible debt first.
   - Pay off personal debts before you retire.
3. Develop or fine-tune your investment strategy:
   - Save up for emergencies (minimum 3 months' income), or make sure that your business's cash flow will be able to maintain your personal income stream.
   - Set your financial goals for retirement.
   - Tailor your investment strategy/risk level to your life stage.
   - Assess your investment performance at least once a year.
   - Make sure that you are investing some of the money you take out of the business.
4. Minimize your taxes:
   - Get good advice! There are lots of tax deductions, credits, and strategies — get a good financial advisor to show you what's available.
   - You are in the unique position of being able to control what your RRSP contribution can be, so manage your earned income to allow a reasonable contribution, then contribute as much as you are allowed.
5. Protect yourself, your family, and your business:
   - Match your insurance to your needs (make sure you have enough disability coverage to replace any lost income before you retire).
   - Keep your business and personal finances separate.
   - Make sure your family will remain financially secure if you die or your spouse dies.
   - Ensure you have a shareholders' agreement or partnership agreement if there are other owners of your business.
   - Protect your estate from over-taxation and ensure it is distributed as quickly as possible and according to your wishes.

- Calculate whether you'll be able to put aside enough money to meet your goals in the time you've set to achieve them. You might have to make some changes now, for future benefit.

After you have made your plan and put it into action, two more stages follow:

- Monitor your progress. This means doing a net-worth assessment at least annually by adding up your assets and subtracting your debts. When you're young, you do an assessment primarily to establish the habit. Later on, the assessment tells you how you're doing and may raise an important warning flag or give you good cause to pat yourself on the back.
- Every now and then, reassess your objectives. A big event such as marriage, divorce, or receiving an inheritance makes the need to do so obvious. So does a big upturn or downturn in your business fortunes. Your situation keeps evolving over time, even without big events. Keep in touch with yourself.

Giving Yourself a Good Life

Living the good life is more than just spending on the things that you enjoy. It's also giving yourself freedom from the stress of worrying how you'll keep a roof over your head and your business prospering. By having a savings plan, you can minimize the stress of living.

Saving is a way of striking a pre-emptive blow at unforeseen events. Putting away a percentage of your earnings each month in a designated emergency account can soften the blow. As a business owner, you might have an alternative: making sure that the business is strong enough financially to carry your personal finances through rough times. It's hard enough dealing with business worries

LIFE EXPECTANCY

If you are a healthy, non-smoking Canadian between 45 and 55 years of age, you can expect to live into your early 80s. This means that even if you retire as late as age 65, which fewer people are doing these days, your retirement fund will have to last you at least 15 years. If you retire at 55, you will need enough income to last you 25 years, almost as long as you worked! Of course, no one can predict how long they'll live, but when it comes to providing for your retirement years, optimism is also pragmatism.

and keeping your personal finances balanced without adding to it the nightmare of not having something to fall back on if you need it. Planning ahead and creating contingencies are ways of having a good life, even when things don't go according to plan.

Business Succession and Retirement Goals

All of these decisions — when to retire and what to do with your business when you do — are closer than you think. You need to have a clear picture of your destination if you're to get there. It might be hard to be specific right now, but it's important to develop a sense of what you believe you'll want and need. Here are some of the kinds of things you might want to be doing:

Business Succession Goals
- realizing the real value of your business in a sale
- winding down your business painlessly
- transferring the business to a relative, co-owner, employee, or friend who has been trained to run it

Retirement Goals
- maintaining your pre-retirement standard of living
- travelling
- working, consulting
- continuing your education
- buying a vacation/second home
- leaving an inheritance
- spending time doing volunteer work or donating to charities
- taking up long-abandoned hobbies
- learning new sports, such as golf, skiing, sailing — these can be costly

You don't want the end of your work life to be the beginning of either family strife or a declining standard of living. Good communication with family members is key, as is sound financial planning. It's important to work out what you're going to need to live on, and although there's no magic formula, you should take three factors into consideration:

1. the number of years between now and retirement,
2. what you believe you'll need to live on per year, and
3. that figure adjusted for inflation.

We'll go into more detail about RRSPs in Chapters 3 and 4.

Goals for Increasing Your Net Worth

When you make a list of your life goals, increasing your net worth should be somewhere near the top. An increased net worth can translate into many of the good things in life — better home, early retirement, travel. So now it's time to make out a list of your goals for increasing your net worth before you retire. As you'll see, some of the things on the list will involve paying off debt; others will involve buying assets, and maybe even incurring some more debt in the process. Your list might look something like this:

- I want to pay off my mortgage.
- I want the business to grow.
- I want to pay off my credit card debt.
- I want to buy a new home/vacation property/car.
- I want to increase my money and financial independence through investments.

These topics are all discussed in greater depth in the chapters to come.

YOUR LIFE GOALS

Only you can identify your life goals and priorities. Do this first: everything else depends on it. Once you know what's most important in your life, you can seek help in identifying the financial goals and strategies that will let you shape the life you want.

THE BASIC PHILOSOPHY

At least once a year, assess your personal financial situation, as well as your long-term and short-term financial goals. Establish a realistic and comfortable plan to achieve those goals. Implement your plan, and stick with it. You don't need to know everything yourself. Use a financial advisor the same way you would use a physician — to take advantage of their expertise to ensure your financial health.

WHAT'S YOUR FINANCIAL HEALTH?

GOOD SYMPTOMS

- You know your net worth (including the value of your business), you know when you want to retire, and you've set your financial goals to get there.
- You've set up a regular savings program to ensure you steadily direct money toward those goals. Nothing fancy, just something that suits you and your goals.
- You've protected yourself against disaster with an emergency fund and an insurance policy.
- You plan to pay off all your debts by the time you retire.
- You have a will.
- You're maxing out your RRSP contribution. If you took money out to buy a house, you've replaced it in time to avoid paying tax.
- You always save enough for tax time and emergencies.
- If incorporated you choose between being paid a dividend, a salary, or a combination of the two so that the total tax paid is minimized and RRSP contribution limit is maximized.
- You prepare your financial statements on time.
- You have a shareholders' or partners' agreement in place if you are not the sole owner of the business.
- You have a plan in place for your business when you retire or die.

BAD SYMPTOMS

- You're living from week to week, unprepared for a rainy day.
- You don't balance your accounts. In fact, you don't even know how much is in each of your accounts, and the cash stability of your business is a constant worry to you.
- You have no savings, assets, or insurance in case of emergencies. It would be nice to have some, but it never works out.
- You're gaining debt using credit cards and loans, and maybe even skipping debt payments. The total is growing, not shrinking.
- You don't have a will.
- You can't afford to max out your RRSP; you may have even taken money out of your RRSP and never paid it back.
- You can't afford your monthly, quarterly or yearly tax bills.
- You are using your savings to pay the business's bills.
- You mix business and personal loans.
- Your financial statements consist of an old shoebox that you give to a bookkeeper when it starts to overflow.
- You sense family members are jockeying for position to take over the family business when you retire or die.

The Big Three

For the greatest possible financial strength as you build your life, follow these three simple principles:

1. Pay off high-cost, non-deductible personal debts first.
2. Start saving (if you haven't already) and accumulating assets for your retirement.
3. Minimize your taxes by using all available deductions, credits, and strategies, both business and personal.

It may not be glamorous, but over time these principles are powerful. The trick is to work out how to stay faithful to them as you make your way through the surprises and changes of life. That's where you'll need to devise strategies and systems, make trade-offs, juggle priorities, and the like. But if you stick to the three principles, many other choices become clearer. The principles will be discussed in more detail later in the book.

GOOD VS BAD DEBT

Your parents may have told you that all debt is bad; but that's not always true.

Good debt: This is debt that works for you by building your assets, such as a business operating loan or even borrowing to max out your RRSP. Some types of debt are even tax-deductible.

Bad debt: This is debt you acquire through overspending, such as borrowing for that wine tour in France you can't really afford. High-cost debt is also bad debt. The worst kind of bad debt is the kind you rack up on your credit card.

Yesterday, Today, and Tomorrow

There's an old joke about the city slicker who gets lost on a small country road and asks a farmer for directions. "If I wanted to get there," says the farmer, "I wouldn't start from here." Somehow that attitude finds its way into personal finance and becomes a major obstacle. "Sure, I want to achieve that goal," it runs, "but this isn't the right time to start."

Look at it another way: this is the only time to start! If you're at the beginning of your life and using most of your resources to launch a business, or if you're entrenched in your field and reaping the benefits of your hard work, today can still be the first day of the rest of your financial life.

But the most important aspect of this financial planning, like exercise, is to start! It doesn't matter how close you are to retiring — even if you're starting only now, there's still time to make your finances work for you. You don't ever want to look back on these years with regret that you should have done something, anything, for your retirement.

You and the Experts

Many experts are out there to advise you, explain things to you, and provide you with products and services. They range from stockbrokers to financial advisors, accountants, portfolio managers, insurance agents, and lawyers.

If you already have a financial expert you use, are you happy with what you are getting? As a small business owner, you probably already have your share of advisors around you. Don't assume your accountant or your lawyer can advise you best on every topic. Seek an expert financial advisor for your personal finances. Experts want your business, so it

NO MORE YO-YO FINANCIAL PLANNING!

* Kick the starvation-diet approach, and start enjoying yourself. Starvation — financial or otherwise — doesn't work. A common-sense approach does.
* Make financial awareness part of your daily lifestyle.
* Have a balanced financial diet: earn, spend, and save. Monitor results. Adjust as appropriate, but keep all three components in the mix.
* Remember: every healthy diet includes treats. Just don't overindulge.
* Think about your retirement goals, and build in activities now that will safeguard them.
* Don't be afraid to ask! You wouldn't do your own surgery or defend yourself in court. Professional advisors working with a reputable firm can help you plan and achieve your goals.

PLAN, PLAN, PLAN

Solid finances mean a solid lifestyle. Start taking greater control of your finances. You can do this by planning. Pre-authorized payment plans, investment plans, and retirement plans all mean greater lifestyle flexibility in the long run.

pays to shop around to find out which one will best suit your needs. Choose your financial expert the same way that you would pick your doctor or dentist. Friends' recommendations can help, but also check credentials and listen to your instincts. You need to find someone you feel comfortable with and trust. And, obviously, you need someone who has experience with the personal finances of a small business owner. Many financial advisors are also self-employed, so they have first-hand knowledge of your special challenges, fears, and opportunities.

Not everyone charges for providing financial advice. Often (like travel agents) the advisor is paid by the distributor of financial products. No matter how carefully you pick and how confident you are in your "normal" life, you may feel tongue-tied when you actually sit down with the financial expert. Here's how to get the best from the meeting:

- Do your homework. Fill in any forms you've been given in advance, take any papers you have been asked to supply, and write out the questions you want answered during the meeting. Be prepared to provide details of all your family finances. It may make you uncomfortable at first, but advisors need all the information to do the best job for you.
- Expect the expert to have done his or her homework as well. Is he or she ready for the meeting? Familiar with your file and background material? Equipped with everything needed to carry out the day's agenda?
- Listen carefully. Ask questions whenever you want more information, or when you don't understand what your advisor is saying. It's not up to you to guess: it's up to the expert to be clear. Professionals will welcome your questions because they want you to understand. Be suspicious of those who brush you off.
- Take notes. Things that seem clear at the time may become blurred in your memory later.
- Cover every topic that was on your list, but don't waste time. Check to see if you are being charged by the hour, but even if you're not, it's courteous to stay on topic.
- Do any necessary follow-up, and make sure that the expert does too.

Above all, remember that the decisions are ultimately up to you. It's your life and your money. Experts can advise and help, but you are in charge. This is a responsibility, as well as a right.

THERE'S NO TIME LIKE THE PRESENT

Now's the time to look at how your assets are allocated so that you can maximize your pre-retirement wealth building.

Summary

Unlike a lot of people out there, you have more than a passing acquaintance with managing money. If you didn't, your business would have been dust long before now. What might be new to you, however, is making sure that you're looking out for yourself as well as your business, and planning your personal finances in such a way that the two sides of your life remain in healthy balance. Striking that balance begins with asking yourself a few questions that will keep the rest of your financial planning on track:

- How can I balance the needs of my business with the needs of my family and our future?
- What do I need, both in the short term and the long term?
- What kinds of things do I want in the short and long term?
- How can I prioritize those needs and wants?
- Do I have special stage-of-life needs?
- Do I know enough about taxes, investments, and strategies to do this without a professional advisor?
- How can I apply the principles of good personal finance to my business?
- How can I match my healthy saving (and spending) habits with my lifestyle and financial goals?

Don't forget to assess your financial situation at least once a year, or to reassess your long-term and short-term financial goals periodically and whenever you encounter a major change in your life (due to marriage, divorce, a death in the family, etc). Establish a realistic and comfortable plan to achieve those goals. Then, it's just a question of getting to it: after all, the plan's no good if it's only a plan!

ONE MORE TIME:
THE BIG THREE PRINCIPLES

1. Pay off high-cost, non-deductible personal debts first.
2. Start saving (if you haven't already) and accumulating assets for your retirement.
3. Minimize your taxes by using all available deductions, credits, and strategies, both business and personal.

Assets and Liabilities

Whether or not you've thought about it, you probably have a conscious (or unconscious) financial plan. But how do you give that plan some direction? Or reassess it when your circumstances change? Your family may now have two incomes, but it may also have double the expenses. How do you adjust you expectations to fit your changing situation? Let's take a look at some typical situations.

Maggie

Maggie, 49, just celebrated the final payment on her car loan, but now she's wondering if she should be finding out directions to the poorhouse. She's a family physician with a nurse and a secretary on the payroll, and she figures the practice has been grossing about $170,000 a year for the last few years. After payroll, deductions, and taxes, however, her take-home is more like $50,000, and with a mortgage, new cuts to health care, rising secretarial costs, two children who need braces, clothes, and schoolbooks ... things aren't as rosy in life as they are on paper. Besides,

Maggie is a single mother now. She's seriously starting to wonder how to provide for her children's futures without mortgaging her own and without damaging the practice she's worked so hard to build up.

Gord and Sally

Gord, 60, and Sally, 50, bought a bookstore 10 years ago, and so far, so good. They specialize in cookbooks and children's books, and their staff of six are known for their expertise. But margins are small — a book they sell for $10 costs them $7.15 to purchase from the distributor, and videos, magazines, and the Internet claim more and more of people's leisure time. They're wondering if they shouldn't change direction a little, and maybe trade one wall of shelf space for a video rack. Even if it brings in another 10 percent, it will be worth it. They have two children, but only one education left to pay for, since the eldest is already articling at a law firm. Gord and Sally still have a few more years left on their mortgage payments, but Gord's insurance premiums seem to rise almost daily as he continues to chain-smoke. Of course, there's always the worry that another franchise big box store might appear down the block and make their lives impossible, but they're trying to be optimistic. Their combined income is about $82,000, but Gord and Sally's investments are scattered and need to be reassessed, and Gord (who's thinking of slowing down pretty soon, maybe even retiring) only manages to get about $200 into his RRSP every month, and he's a little worried about his own future.

John

John is rich. He sensed the change in communication technology about 15 minutes before anyone else, and as a result he got the jump on everyone. Now he runs a digital design firm with 60 employees, who do everything from designing content for new Web-based broadcast companies to creating computer-based live presentations, to making quarterly reports on CD-ROM for some of Canada's largest corporations. Keeping one step ahead takes up almost all of John's time (not to mention all the energy it takes to woo away the best talent from competitors), and he looks 10 years older than his 41 years. He's been immensely successful in all areas but one: he keeps his money in the financial equivalent of a mattress. He has a bunch of savings accounts and chequing accounts bursting at the seams with money, all of it earning next to nothing. John doesn't have an RRSP. He doesn't have a mortgage either (he bought the house for cash). His business savvy tells him that today's news is tomorrow's bird-cage lining: he's seen lots of people go from boom to bust, and finally he's wondering if he shouldn't start taking better care of his money.

The Future Begins in the Present

Maggie, Gord and Sally, and John all have hopes and fears rooted in their business lives. They are not as confident as they would like to be, they don't feel fully in control of where they are or where they're going, and they know that looking after themselves and their families in the future depends on decisions they make today.

You may be feeling exactly the same way. How can anyone predict his or her own financial future, especially given the instability of various marketplaces and the fact that small business is a pretty volatile place to be. Today you're the next big thing; tomorrow you're yesterday's fad. While no one can give you the financial-planning equivalent of a crystal ball, there are ways to figure out what your various options are and what's possible for you. The trick is to start off by figuring out where you are today.

What Are You Worth?

There isn't one single profile of a small business owner. Maybe you are starting your first company fresh out of university, or you've got lots of experience under your belt and you're in your prime earning years, or you could be just approaching retirement. Whatever the case, your business training has taught you to keep good tabs on the value of your company, but do you know how much you are worth personally? What major assets do you have? Remember that a major asset at age 20 might be a state-of-the-art stereo, while a major asset for someone who has been running a business for decades would be their business, home, or vacation property. You probably also have some debts, such as credit card bills, car loans, or a mortgage. So, are you in the red or in the black? Are you building your assets or frittering away your money? Can you afford your debts? Will you have paid off your debts and maximized your assets by the time you retire (even if it seems a long way away)? Do you have a plan for asset building? To find out your true worth, you'll need to review your assets and liabilities.

Assets

People can have strange ideas of what constitutes an asset if they confuse them with things that have sentimental, or personal, value. Your employees are obviously (hopefully) assets, but what we mean here are the things that can be thought of in terms of value in the marketplace. There are two basic kinds of assets: personal-use assets and investment assets. Investment assets include cash, stocks, mutual funds, and bonds — and the money you have tied up in your business. We will discuss them in Chapter 8. Common types of personal use assets are:

- principal residence, summer residence (could also be an investment)
- appliances (this includes your personal, not business, computer, although its rate of depreciation means it won't be an asset for long)
- vehicles
- furniture
- camera equipment
- jewellery

Liabilities

When you purchase assets, it is important to remember the flip side: liabilities. This is the debt you incur to acquire your assets. Unless you have our friend John's wallet, you probably won't be able to pay for everything in cash. As you'll see, taking on debt to acquire assets is a normal practice that can work in your favour, as long as you do it sensibly. Common liabilities are:

- mortgages
- loans
- lines of credit (personal)

- operating lines (business)
- credit cards
- unpaid bills

Whose Net Worth?

Before you fill out your net worth sheet below, think about whose net worth you are calculating. Are you calculating your net worth or both yours and your spouse's? If you jointly share possessions (such as the family home and cars) and debts (such as mortgage and the car loan), you may want to calculate a household, rather than personal, net worth. On the other hand, if you want to keep tabs on what's yours, you may want to do separate net-worth statements.

Calculating Your Net Worth

Now that you know what assets and liabilities are, take a look at your own. Fill out the following form to find out whether you come out in the red or black.

ASSETS

Your business (the next chapter discusses
how to value your business) $ _____

Deposit accounts
Institution   amount
                                                                $ _____
_____ $ _____
_____   total $ _____

Life insurance (cash surrender value)
Company   amount
                                                                $ _____
_____ $ _____
_____   total $ _____

Pensions
Company   amount
                                                                $ _____
_____ $ _____
_____   total $ _____

Non-registered investments
(stocks, funds, GICs, bonds, mortgages held,
business interests, etc.)
Institution   amount
                                                                $ _____
_____ $ _____
_____   total $ _____

RRSPs (including spousal RRSPs)
Institution   amount
                                                                $ _____
_____ $ _____
_____   total $ _____

Real estate (home, summer home, other)   amount
                                                                $ _____
_____ $ _____
_____   total $ _____

Other assets (equipment, furnishings, jewellery, art)   amount
                                                                $ _____
_____ $ _____
_____   total $ _____

Accounts receivable (loans made to your business
or to family and friends, tax refunds owing)   amount
                                                                $ _____
_____ $ _____
_____   total $ _____

TOTAL ASSETS $ _____

LIABILITIES

Mortgages
Lender   amount owing
_____ $ _____

Loans
1. Lender   amount owing
_____ $ _____

2. Lender   amount owing
_____ $ _____

3. Lender   amount owing
_____ $ _____

Accounts payable
(credit cards, taxes, outstanding bills)   _____

                                                _____

                                                _____

                                                    total $ _____

Other debt (guarantees, personal obligations)   total $ _____

TOTAL LIABILITIES $ _____

NET WORTH

This is the big one. Subtract your total liabilities from your total assets.
This is your net worth.

TOTAL ASSETS $ _____

TOTAL LIABILITIES   – $ _____

TOTAL NET WORTH   = $ _____

What Your Assessment Really Means

If you are in good financial health, you should have come out in the black. But you may not be as flush as you thought you were. You may have come out in the red if you have several loans to pay off. To figure out whether you have too many liabilities, look at your monthly payments for those liabilities. If they are more than 40 percent of your net personal income, you may want to skip ahead to our discussion of debt management in Chapter 9. But before you have an anxiety attack, keep in mind that your net worth assessment does have a margin for error. For example, if you own a house, a drop in its market value could put you in the red, even though you're not planning to sell. Or a real estate bubble could put your net worth artificially high. Whatever your net worth, you will want to increase it. Here are two simple ways of doing that:

- Curb your spending habits.
- Invest wisely. If you do this, your money should work harder and give you a better rate of return.

APPRECIABLE VS DEPRECIABLE

When you are making a major purchase, such as buying a vacation property, a computer or a car, consider whether the asset is likely to appreciate or depreciate in value. If it is likely to depreciate, how long do you expect to own the asset? Do you expect to resell it? If so, will the difference in value be more than paid for by your use of the asset? Or are you better off renting? If it is likely to appreciate, how long can you expect to wait before you resell it? Would your money be better spent renting the object and putting the difference into a high-yield mutual fund?

Financial Habits

Cutting expenses is only the most obvious way of squeezing savings out of your budget. Take a look at the following list of habits you can either develop or squelch to make the most of your income. Many of these ideas are further explained in later chapters.

HABITS THAT HELP

✔ Working out a budget for the year, and sticking to it.
✔ Paying yourself first by starting, or increasing, your automatic savings plan. Or better yet, investigate a group RRSP plan for your business.
✔ Planning for your needs once you retire. You're going to have new activities and probably some new spending habits, too. Looking ahead to prepare for these changes is an excellent strategy.
✔ Looking at how you use your credit cards. Are you able to pay them off each month? Are you at risk of having to use your RRSP to pay off your cards once you retire? If so, perhaps you should consider using your debit card instead. (Credit cards usually cost 16 to 18 percent interest a month; department store cards cost 25 to 30 percent a year.)
✔ Becoming a smart consumer. Research major purchases before buying. Check consumer magazines for repair records and ratings of cars and appliances. Shop around for the best deal (this goes for things like auto insurance, too).
✔ Looking into borrowing if you can't make the maximum RRSP contribution this year. (Often, the cost of borrowing is more than outweighed by the income you will make from your compounding RRSP.) (See Chapter 4.)
✔ Making sure you've put some money aside each month to pay your taxes.

HABITS THAT HURT

✗ Buying things you don't really need.

✗ Keeping your money in a low-interest account and letting inflation eat away at it.

✗ Missing the RRSP deadline because you don't have the cash for a lump sum payment. (This also means you'll pay extra income tax, so get in the habit of contributing monthly).

✗ Waiting for the RRSP deadline to contribute. This means you'll earn less income. Contributions made throughout the year earn income that ends up compounding on a tax-deferred basis.

✗ Signing up for more credit cards than necessary. Just because a company sends you an application for a gold card doesn't mean you have to bite. Getting closer to retirement, enticements to get into debt are temptations to be avoided.

ARE YOU MAXIMIZING YOUR BUSINESS EARNINGS?

Since you pay yourself, your income is intimately related to how your business is doing. So the big question is: have you found all the efficiencies you can in your business in order to maximize what you can afford to pay yourself? Whether it's a matter of managing your inventory intelligently, using your staff efficiently, or finding places where your money is evaporating (among dozens of other approaches), your personal income is, as a small business owner, at least partly up to your own ingenuity.

Conversely, some business owners are so obsessed with minimizing the tax they have to pay that they end up with no personal income — which means they can't contribute to an RRSP and won't contribute to CPP/QPP. Such short-term tax savings can devastate your personal finances come retirement time.

AUTOMATIC DEBIT

Find some way to make your RRSP contribution — group or personal — before you have a chance to spend it. Automatic debit services are an excellent way of ensuring that you save for the future. And you won't miss the money, because the deduction is happening out of the corner of your eye. (See the section on group RRSPs in Chapter 4.)

Be Prepared

Now that you have a sense of where you're starting from, where you're going, and what you want, mapping out a course should be much easier. But just as you consulted with professionals in your field before you opened your business, you should do some research on your personal investments before you start playing with your hard-earned money.

At some point you'll need to talk to some financial professionals (think of them as business consultants, if you like), but before you get to that step, this book will help familiarize you as much as possible with this new territory and the local language and customs. After all, making your way through the myriad of financial services and products on the market can be overwhelming at first. This book will help answer important questions such as: What's a guaranteed investment certificate? What is the right kind of insurance for me? How does the stock market work? Are mutual funds any safer than buying individual stocks? What is the best way to pass on my business?

Remember that knowledge is power. The more you learn about personal finances, the more confident you'll feel in making decisions that can affect your life for years to come. But remember, too, that the financial world is complex, and you should consider taking advantage of a professional's knowledge and experience. Most people are just too busy with their business and their family to keep up-to-date with all of the latest investment options.

Summary

If you've done a self-assessment and re-prioritized your goals, congratulations! You've taken the first steps to a new financial future. The next step — actually doing something about that huge credit card balance, or your inability to leave a business-supply store empty-handed — may be a little more challenging.

That's because all this may not be forever. You may have children, or be planning to have children. Or maybe you're thinking of actually retiring but haven't started to think about how until now. Your mind has, understandably, been occupied with getting your business up and running, or keeping it running. But as all the characters in this chapter are realizing, the future is coming, and soon. Even for John, who enjoyed a profligate twenties, it's not too soon to consider what lies ahead. No matter what stage of life you're in, or how your business is performing, if you don't start saving for the future now, you're more likely to "enjoy" tin years, not golden ones.

So do something today for the person you'll be in just a few years. It's up to you now to determine whether you end up stuck in a cramped one-room apartment heating up beans on a hot-plate, or whether you get to sit on the deck of your paid-off cottage, sipping fine wine and planning a cruise to Barbados.

QUICK RECAP

1. **Identify the goals that you want to work toward.**

2. **Assess your net worth.**

3. **Start exchanging your bad financial habits for good ones.**

CHAPTER 3

Retiring in Style

Sources of Retirement Income

Your business is going gangbusters, you're having the time of your life, and the last thing you want to think about is your retirement. But one of the reasons why you're working so hard now is that you want to retire in style later. The only way to do that is to plan how you're going to maintain an income long after you stop going into the shop every day. And, unlike people who are employed by a company, you don't have the safety net of a company pension plan. As a business owner, you are always looking after your own needs, but that will become even more important when you retire. Luckily, there are many different sources of retirement income that you can live on during your retirement. The main ones are outlined below.

Reaping What You've Sown

Maybe retirement is just around the corner; maybe it's still a long way off. No matter how many more years you intend to be working, what you plan to do with your business is a serious concern that requires plenty of forethought. Chances are your decision will affect many more people than just you, and if part of your desire is to see your business continue without you, then how you plan is very important. As you look toward retirement, there are three main options.

Sell

Just as when you started your business (or purchased it), there are legions of people looking for good opportunities. Your good name, the quality of your product, your long-standing presence in a certain marketplace, your physical plant — all of these are reasons someone may wish to pick up where you want to leave off. You may find potential purchasers within your business (past or present employees), among your competitors, among your suppliers, or by advertising. Selling a business is a complicated procedure, and not one we can get into with much detail here, but some of the up side includes realizing the value of your company, avoiding the complications of closing shop, and continuing to provide for loyal customers through the continuation of the business. Another benefit to selling is that the income generated by the sale of your business could provide a portion of your retirement income. That is, in addition to your healthy RRSP.

VALUING YOUR BUSINESS

Obviously, you value your business highly. But how do you come to a fair price when selling? There are many different elements to consider:

- outstanding accounts receivable (which the purchaser may be buying)
- fixed and movable assets (fixtures vs furnishings, buildings and land, if you own any)
- inventory
- Intangibles, such as the business's reputation, customer base, existing licences, and trademarks, among many others

Clearly, there is no single method. A selling agent might be able to help you value the business, but be prepared to part with a percentage. You might be better off researching how similar businesses in your area have been valued, and then relying on old-fashioned, hard negotiations to get your best price. Or better yet, consider hiring a certified business valuator.

Wind down

In some cases, you may be the main reason the business exists. It may not be possible, for instance, to sell your consulting business because you're the main asset. Or, as a doctor or lawyer, you may be concerned that your clients won't get the same level of service from any of the propects who are willing to buy your practice. You may also wish to avoid the bother of seeking a buyer for a business that would be logical to wind down or that you don't believe would attract a buyer. Winding down involves selling or disposing of the remaining inventory, giving proper notice to landlords and customers, and in the case of incorporated companies, doing a certain amount of legal paperwork. Be prepared for the effort required (physical and emotional) to close a business.

Pass the business on

Of the three options, this is the most sensitive one, but it may also be the most satisfying. There may be relatives or employees who want to take over your business when you're ready to retire. But to effect this, careful planning must be undertaken to make the transition a smooth one. The owner of a small business should plan ahead and value the business fairly. Will it be possible for the family members or senior employees to continue to run it? Paradoxically, having spent a lifetime building up a business, the owner (thinking of the security of his or her dependants) may find it best to have the business sold before the end of their life instead of passing it on. Looking ahead is the key. There may be no one in your family or in your employ who can realistically do what you have done. After all, you're the manager, and you make the decisions. Can others do as well? Be realistic. Some types of business are more likely to be retained in the family. These are operations that have a multi-generational history, where the maintenance of tradition, customer loyalty, and family pride all play a part in encouraging the survivors to maintain the business. Then, too, the building of a successful business may be seen so much as a life work that the family will want to continue it. Farming operations are a special case. Several generations may have been involved in operating the farm, all sharing the same dedication and acquiring the land and equipment necessary to make an agricultural business flourish. The shared purpose of more than one generation is required.

KEEPING FAMILY HARMONY

Major family events, like the passing on of a business, or the execution of a will, can be trying times. In either case, the key to reducing stress and conflict is to make nothing a surprise. Long before you retire, discuss with your family some options concerning the business. Discuss with your spouse or children the possibility that one or some of them will take over the business. Or why, for instance, you might want to wind it down or sell it. Go over the ins and outs of each option and gauge the needs and desires of members of your family. The same goes for a will: the last thing your heirs need is a shock in the lawyer's office. Consider discussing with your family their wishes for the dispersal of your worldly goods. Remember: you can't take back anything you've done in life after you're gone.

RRSPs and RRIFs

We'll go into much more detail on Registered Retirement Savings Plans (RRSPs) in Chapter 4, but for now what you need to know is that they're your most dependable partner when it comes to providing for yourself in retirement. You must "mature" your RRSP no later than the end of the calendar year in which you turn 69, so you must select a retirement income program. This program could be a life annuity (with or without a guaranteed term), a term-certain annuity to age 90, or a RRIF, which has a required minimum payout. We talk a lot more about RRIFs in our book *Retire Ready*.

Annuities

Annuities are contracts that promise a future income stream provided by a financial institution (such as an insurance company or a trust company) out of a lump sum you provide. Usually a monthly payment is made to you out of this fund. There are two main types of annuities: life annuities, which pay regularly for the rest of your life (and are generally available through insurance companies), and term-certain annuities. Consult a financial advisor about the fine print on both.

Non-Registered Investments

Another source of income is, of course, any investments you hold out-side of an RRSP. These might be stocks and bonds, real estate, or other assets that could provide you with an income.

Company Pension Plans

These are employer-sponsored retirement plans that are registered with Revenue Canada. The company creates the pension plan. Like any employee, you can join the plan. The company must be incorporated and you must be receiving T4 salary.

Individual Pension Plans (IPPs)

Individual pension plans (IPPs) provide annual income after retire-ment up to a maximum specified by the Income Tax Act. In many cases, corporations can make a larger contribution towards the IPP than owner-managers can towards their RRSP. There are a few finan-cial institutions that can help you set up and manage an IPP. The only down side to these plans is that they are available only to incorporat-ed businesses and they are expensive to administer. If you are not incorporated, your main option, outside of CPP/QPP and OAS, is to maximize your RRSP contributions.

IPPs are best suited to individuals who are over 50 years of age and will, each year until retirement, have an annual income of more than $80,000. For most owner-managers who have an IPP, the amount of their pension contributions has reduced the allowable RRSP contribu-tion to zero.

Government Sources

The Canada and Quebec pension plans (CPP/QPP) cover Canadians who are either employees or self-employed. Retirement benefits depend on your record of contributions and when you start taking benefits. You can start as early as 60 or wait as late as 70. For each month you claim before you turn 65, your payment is reduced by 0.5

percent (6 percent per year). For every month you wait after your 65th birthday, your payment increases by 0.5 percent. If you have a financial advisor, talk to him or her about whether you might benefit from starting the CPP/QPP early. (That way you can keep your RRSP tax-sheltered for longer.) You must apply for this benefit, so plan to contact Human Resources Development Canada or the Caisse de dépôt et placement de Québec a few months before you want to retire.

Old Age Security (OAS)/Seniors' Benefit

Big changes are afoot. Starting in 2001, a new Seniors' Benefit will take effect for anyone 65 or older.

The new Seniors' Benefit proposes to replace OAS, Guaranteed Income Supplement (GIS) and Spouse's Allowance (SPA) as well as the pension and age tax credits. Unlike the OAS, it will be tax-free, but the amount you will be entitled to will be based on a sliding scale measured against your income. The higher the income, the smaller the benefit.

Your Retirement Age

First you'll need to know when you're likely to retire. Most pension plans, including the CPP/QPP, specify age 65, and most Canadians still consider that the "normal" retirement age. If you go strictly by the government's RRSP book, your retirement age is 69. You can retire any time you can afford to. You cannot make contributions to your own RRSP after the end of the year in which you turn 69, although you can still make spousal RRSP contributions if you have contribution room and if your spouse is under age 70. You can preserve your tax deferral by converting it into either a RRIF or an annuity.

How Much Does a Retired Person Need?

Although you may need $40,000 a year now, you'll likely not need quite as much when you retire. For one thing, you probably won't be contributing to your RRSP. You will probably have paid off your mortgage and sent your children to school. There will usually be fewer big expenses left to pay off, but sometimes you need more than before in the early retirement years, to fund long-delayed goals like elaborate trips.

But remember that having enough to live on when you retire usually means more than just paying your own expenses. You may be trying to keep enough of an estate that it will benefit your heirs. Then again, you may never have married and have only a cat as a dependent. Whatever the future may hold for you, be realistic about how much you're going to need. Better to have too much than too little. If you calculate your retirement needs at about 70 percent of your current income, adjusted for inflation, you'll have a good ballpark figure for what you'll need.

The Fear of Falling Short

You may be thinking: at this rate, I'll only have 55 percent of my pre-retirement income to live on! What do I do? There are a couple of tactics. One is to take the advice in this book to heart and learn ways to maximize your retirement income. This might mean passing a little now on the extras to free up some cash for your RRSP. Another tactic is to make retirement a time when you learn to live with less. But if you have a choice (and you do), it's wiser to enrich your future now rather than deal with the consequences later.

Reality Check

Now take a look at the following table. It shows you how many months it would take to save various amounts using different monthly contributions to your RRSP. A common fear about saving for retirement is that the savings won't be worth as much by the time you retire. However, you will be investing your savings with an objective to get a return that's higher than the inflation rate, so your purchasing power will grow. Remember, $1,000,000 may not be worth as much when you retire as it is now, but it is sure to be worth a lot more than zero dollars, which is what you'll have if you never get started on your savings.

NUMBER OF MONTHS IT WOULD TAKE TO SAVE

AMOUNT PER MONTH	$1,000	$2,500	$5,000	$7,500	$10,000
$50	19	44	77	104	127
$75	13	31	56	77	96
$100	10	24	44	61	77
$150	7	16	31	44	56
$200	5	12	24	35	44
$250	4	10	19	28	36
$500	2	5	10	15	19

Note: This table assumes a rate of return of 8 percent. The monthly contribution is invested at the beginning of the month, and interest is compounded monthly. No taxes or inflation are included in these calculations.

Adjusting for Inflation

If there was no inflation, you could simply multiply what you think you'll need to live on by the number of years you hope to live after retirement, and that would be what you'd need to save in an RRSP. The chart below should give you some idea of how inflation forces you to earn more in order to keep your dollar's buying power.

IMPACT OF INFLATION ON PURCHASING POWER

Annual Rate of Inflation	Value Today	5 Years	10 Years	15 Years	20 Years	30 Years
3%	1,000	863	744	642	554	412
4%	1,000	822	676	555	456	308
5%	1,000	784	614	481	377	231
6%	1,000	747	558	417	312	174
7%	1,000	713	508	362	258	131
8%	1,000	681	463	315	215	99
9%	1,000	650	422	275	178	75
10%	1,000	621	386	239	149	57
11%	1,000	593	352	209	124	44
12%	1,000	567	322	183	104	33
13%	1,000	543	295	160	87	26

These projections are based on certain assumptions that are believed to be reasonable, but there is no assurance that the actual results will be consistent with this projection. The actual results may vary, perhaps to a material degree, from these projections.

Summary

Even though you are more concerned right now with the continued success of your business, that doesn't mean you shouldn't be planning for your retirement. That entails deciding what to do with your business once your work life is over, as well as figuring our what you need to retire on. Once you know these things, you can put a strong plan in place for taking care of yourself and your family when you retire, and you can continue to expand your business in the present.

QUICK RECAP

1. **Plan ahead for winding down, selling, or passing on your business.**

2. **Calculate how much income you will need to live on in your retirement.**

3. **Take inflation into account when planning for the future.**

4. **Make sure you have various different sources of retirement income.**

From Here to Retirement

Maggie, the 49-year-old family physician, drives a sporty new car and feels as if she has a new lease on life since she and her husband separated. Maggie doesn't work in a crowded office where she can see the junior employees climbing up the corporate ladder, her friends are all much younger than she is (she started medical school when she was 32), and except for minimal RRSP contributions, she never really thinks about retirement. But Maggie's son, who is taking an economics class in high school, recently pointed out to her that she is 16 years away from the normal retirement age in Canada, and has only another 20 years to contribute to her RRSP. Maggie then sat down and figured out how much retirement income she'll need when she gives up her practice, and got the shock of her life.

Does Maggie need to sell the new car? Not at all. Sure, she's behind some people in investing for her retirement, but her house is paid off, she's not in danger of being downsized out of her job, and her ex-husband is reliable with his support payments. If she follows some of the sensible steps outlined in the next few pages, she'll be doing fine.

The Big Save — Getting There from Here

Now that you know how much retirement income you will need, it's time to start socking some of that away. If you invest the right amount of money between now and the time you retire, it should grow to meet your needs by the time you're ready to retire.

How Much More Do You Need?

If you've reviewed your RRSPs and your eligibility for OAS and CPP/QPP, you've probably come to the conclusion that you will need to supplement your retirement income with your own savings. Hopefully you already have an RRSP and are making the maximum contribution before you put any money towards your unregistered investments. To calculate how much you will need to have saved by the time you decide to retire, calculate how much you will need to live on and then subtract any other pension income you expect to be getting. You probably will need help from a financial advisor to do these calculations.

How Long Will It Take You to Save That?

A savings strategy should be a plan that can administer itself. Once you know how much money you'd likely need when you retire, you should calculate how much to put aside per month to get there. Let's assume that you have been contributing moderately to your RRSP since you started your family 20 years ago. With the tax shelter and the compound rate of return, your savings have amounted to $160,000. You are 55 years old. How much do you have to contribute to get your savings up to your goal of $394,000 in 10 years? It is not as daunting as you might think. Your $160,000 will grow to $297,679 if invested at 8 percent a year. You can get to your goal of $394,000 in 10 years by contributing slightly more than $500 a month.

How Do You Save Enough?

No matter what you are saving for, you need to set up a separate savings account. You are less likely to touch savings if they are kept out of your chequing accounts. Wherever you decide to put your savings, this place should have three main traits: it should be accessible, secure, and profitable. The most commonly used place for your funds is a savings account. The money is readily available, but interest rates are often quite low.

Money market mutual funds are often a better short-term savings option. They usually have a higher return than savings accounts.

For long-term investing, money market mutual funds and savings accounts are not the place to be. You need a balanced portfolio of growth and income investments.

The Little Savings Plan That Grew

Unless you live where there are no televisions or magazines, you probably know that the initials RRSP stand for registered retirement savings plan. Every RRSP is registered with Revenue Canada as an authorized savings plan. Building an RRSP is one of the only ways you can shelter your money for the future without losing much of it to taxes. It should be the cornerstone of healthy retirement planning. Each year, the government will allow you to invest money in an RRSP designed to provide you with retirement income. The amount is reduced if you are a member of a registered pension plan. Not only do you pay no tax on the money in your RRSP as it's growing, but your yearly contribution is also tax-deductible. So there is an incentive to invest as much as you can, which will grow over time into a healthy nest egg. Don't overdo it — there are penalties for overcontributing to your RRSP.

Where Can You Buy One?

Before you sign up for an RRSP, do a little comparison shopping. Banks aren't the only places you can buy an RRSP — most financial institutions offer them, including trust companies, credit unions, life insurance companies, investment dealers, and mutual fund companies. You will find that investment dealers and mutual fund companies offer as wide a range of RRSP options as the banks do. Wherever your RRSP is currently registered you may want to ensure you are informed about your alternatives.

Big Business Benefits for the Small Business

We've talked about your own RRSP, but what about your employees, if you have any? Being small doesn't mean being limited. Now a small enterprise with a small workforce can enjoy many of the plans and benefits enjoyed by larger businesses, such as a group RRSP. Your financial advisor can help you set up and administer these plans.

Group plans are an effective way to maximize savings or benefits through a payroll deduction plan. Being deductions from source, they reduce the amount of income tax paid by the employee, and they can be an attractive element of a salary package.

Pension plans

Financial institutions offer a wide variety of individual and group pension plans. Most of these work on the "forced savings" principle, lessening the income tax paid per paycheque. Some to consider are money purchase pension plans (MPPP), shareholder MPPPs, defined benefit pension plans, and individual pension plans (described in Chapter 3). A good financial advisor can help you investigate your options to find the right match for you and your business.

Group registered retirement savings plan (GRRSP)

Employees invest in the GRRSP through the employer, who deducts the employee's contribution from payroll. The contributions can be flexible, and employees are usually involved in investment decisions. These plans can allow for a spousal RRSP, which has the effect of splitting your retirement income, resulting in possible income tax benefits in retirement. Some additional benefits for the small business owner include using employer contributions as a form of year-end bonus payment or profit sharing. The GRRSP can also make a lower salary package more attractive.

Deferred profit sharing plan (DPSP)

This type of program creates a trust fund that enables employees to share in the growth of your business. You make tax-deductible contributions to the plan according to a formula based on your company's profits. A DPSP can serve as a bonus or reward system in lieu of pay increases and can help motivate employee loyalty.

Minimize Your Taxes

Putting part of your income towards an RRSP isn't the only way to reduce your tax bill. Here are a couple more ways you can make your money go further:

Create a spousal RRSP

If you make more money than your spouse, it may make sense to set up and contribute to a spousal RRSP. It is owned by your spouse; however, you receive the tax deduction for the contribution. If your spouse will be in a lower tax bracket when the money is withdrawn in retirement, the income withdrawn from it will be taxed at a lower rate. It also establishes a source of retirement income that can qualify for the pension income credit in the spouse's hands after age 65. Note that if the spousal RRSP is redeemed too soon after the last contribution to any spousal RRSP, the person who got the tax benefit from the contribution may be required to show the redeemed amount as income. Consult a financial advisor to avoid this costly error.

Putting your pension in your RRSP

If you were previously an employee and belonged to a registered pension plan with your employer, you may be able to roll your pension fund into an RRSP. Most vested benefits are locked in, which means that they can't be paid back as a cash refund. They can sometimes be transferred to a locked-in RRSP. This type of RRSP has restrictions on the maximum amount that can be withdrawn annually. Some provinces also have restrictions on the age at which withdrawals can begin. These restrictions ensure that the money is used for retirement income.

Should You Borrow to Buy Your RRSP?

It is a good idea to contribute the maximum amount to your RRSP each year. In February, you should max out your contribution if you haven't already done so. It can be a good strategy to borrow to make your contribution if you don't have enough cash. The interest on the money you borrow isn't tax-deductible, but the cost of borrowing may still be outweighed by the increase in value of your RRSP and the value of your tax deduction. Many financial institutions offer good rates for RRSP loans if you get the RRSP with their company. It is even possible to find a company that will defer repayment of the loan for up to 120 days, enough time to convert your tax refund into a loan payment.

Becoming Your Own RRSP Manager

You probably know that RRSPs are administered through financial institutions, but did you know that you can manage your own RRSP portfolio? A self-directed RRSP involves more work than having a manager look out for your money, and you are entirely responsible for doing your own research and monitoring investments outside of any mutual fund investments. But for some people, they offer a great feeling of accomplishment.

Moreover, there are some types of investments that are open only to self-directed RRSP holders. Be warned though: you have to know what you are doing and what types of investments are available to you, as well as keep abreast of changes that the government makes to RRSP rules. There is no investment advisor or money manager to hold your hand with these plans, so your risk is greater.

Self-directed plans generally have fees attached, often $100 to $150 per plan every year.

The Last Word on RRSPs

They're the best way to shelter your money and defer taxes. Even if you put only tiny amounts into it, you'll be doing yourself more good than if you never bother. There is no down side to RRSPs — they help you now and they help you later.

TALK TO THE EXPERTS

Take advantage of the legions of experts who can advise you about setting up an RRSP, select the right mix of investments, and review it with you on a regular basis.

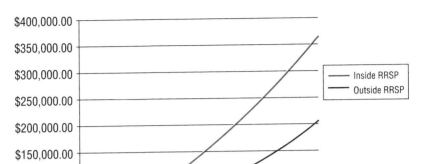

Investing $500 a Month Inside and Outside an RRSP

Note: This graph assumes a rate of return of 8 percent. The monthly contribution is invested at the beginning of the month, and interest is compounded monthly. The inflation rate is 3 percent, and the taxation rate is 28 percent.

Take My Money, Please

The easiest way to stick to your contribution plan is to arrange with your financial institution for a pre-authorized automatic investment plan to debit your account each month. Now you don't have to think about making the investments yourself, and you take advantage of your RRSP contributions working for you earlier in the year.

If your RRSP is invested in a mutual fund, there's another good reason to make regular monthly investments rather than one annual contribution. Making regular investments takes advantage of price fluctuations within your funds. At the end of each year, you'll not only have been compounding your rate of return on 12 separate investments, but you'll have purchased your funds for a price averaged out over the year. This is called dollar-cost averaging. It is discussed in more detail in Chapter 7.)

Summary: The Seven Magic Words

Here's a tidy summary of this chapter, reduced to a list of seven words you could easily stick on your fridge. These are the cornerstones of making your retirement nest-egg grow.

Choose: Set retirement and tax planning goals both for your distant future and your near future.

Plan: Work towards your goals by calculating how much you need to save.

Discipline: Learn to save with regularity. You won't fritter away small amounts now that could add up to big amounts later.

Authorize: Start an automatic payment plan direct to your RRSP.

Maximize: Take advantage of price fluctuations and compound rates of return by making monthly investments into your RRSP.

Listen: Be aware of changes to RRSP legislation, especially if you have a self-directed RRSP.

Live: Try to strike a balance between being diligent and being obsessed. By being happy rather than stressed, you'll have a better chance of being around when it comes time to enjoy all that money you've saved.

CHAPTER 5

Making Sure with Insurance

John, the single workaholic, has insured his business to the hilt, but sees no reason why he himself should be insured. With no family to support, John doesn't see the point in getting life insurance. But John hasn't even thought about what would happen if he got seriously ill and couldn't go to work for an extended period of time. After all, he runs his business almost single-handedly. And what about his parents? They didn't plan for their future as well as John is planning for his, and he now pays half of their rent every month. What would they do if John could no longer provide for them? John doesn't need a lot of insurance coverage, but his financial advisor can help him decide what kind he does need, and can advise him in the future if John gets married and has a family and needs more coverage.

Get Covered

Most people don't like to talk about insurance because it forces them to think about the unimaginable: emergencies with nothing to fall back on, exposure to all manner of legal trouble, and no provisions for your family in the event of your death. Insurance provides you with an invisible safety net and makes it easier to go about your life. It's a necessary part of a financial plan and a sound way of protecting your family and yourself, as well as your business interests.

It may seem obvious, but buy insurance before you need the benefits. The whole point of insurance is to cover your interests — both personal and business — before something happens. Costs can be substantial, though, so weigh the costs of having insurance against the cost of not having it. Generally the financial consequences of not being insured far outweigh the cost of proper coverage. If you wait until you have a medical condition, you may find that your application is denied or that the cost has drastically increased. Or, in the case of business insurance, waiting until someone launches a lawsuit before you purchase a liability package is not conducive to staying in business.

Types of Business Insurance

Your business is like a second family: you have to take similar precautions to protect and provide for it. In the event of your death, insurance will play a major role in smoothing the transition for your business. Here are some of the main types of insurance for small business owners.

Liability insurance

Liability insurance is designed to protect your business from actions brought against it due to negligence causing injury to customers, employees, or the general public. Negligence can encompass any number of acts or omissions leading to injury. Different kinds of businesses use different types of liability insurance. Here are some of the most common:

- Product liability insurance for manufacturers
- Error and omission liability for lawyers, accountants, architects and — insurance agents
- Employer liability for employee safety
- Officers' and directors' liability for the directors of corporations

Property insurance

Property and fire insurance cover your business premises, equipment, and furnishings.

Key person insurance

The sudden death or disability of a key man or woman in a small business often spells disaster for the enterprise. Key person insurance protects against the loss in profitability that often occurs while a replacement is being trained or a strategy is being developed to deal with the key person's death. Life insurance can also be used to repay or reduce business debt if the key person dies.

Business continuation insurance

Also called "business interruption insurance," this type of policy protects against an unforeseen circumstance that temporarily suspends activities. Fire, theft, and flooding are among the interruptions that can be covered to offset expenses and loss of income.

Buy-sell insurance

A buy-sell agreement is a contract in which the various owners of a business agree that if one of them dies or leaves the business for any other reason, the others will purchase his or her interest in the business. The parties to the contract may be partners agreeing to purchase the interest of a partner who dies. They may be a parent and child, where the child wishes to purchase the business on the death of the parent. Buy-sell agreements can also exist between two or more shareholders of a private company who agree to buy each other's shares in the event of death, disability, or disagreement.

When one of the parties to the agreement dies, the buy-sell agreement dictates what happens to the interest of the deceased. Usually the best and most inexpensive way to do this is to ensure that when the buy-sell is established, the parties put into place the appropriate amount of life insurance to provide the survivors with cash to pay for the interest of the deceased. Buy-sell agreements should be considered in consultation with a financial advisor, a lawyer, and an accountant.

Health and disability insurance

All types of business require straightforward protection against sickness and accident. The only questions are "How much?" and "What kind is best for my type of business?"

About 70 percent of Canadian businesses are small businesses with sales of less than $250,000 per year. In such businesses the health and abilities of a very few people affect the continued health of the organization. In general, lack of capable management is the cause of most small business failures, and losses from sickness or accident should be protected against, within reason.

For the sole proprietor, the need is most glaring. Business profits and losses are that person's losses, and everything the proprietor owns is backing up that business. In the very short term, a loyal spouse or devoted employees can keep things on an even keel. But protracted absence from the business will be fatal. There is only one solution — some form of long-term disability insurance. There is a special type of disability insurance available for business owners which would pay fixed costs like rent, power, salaries of employees, etc. And the premiums are tax deductible.

There are as many different health and disability policies as there are small businesses, so it behooves you to shop around to find the policy that best meets the needs of your business.

Group insurance

As with retirement planning, you can offer some group insurance benefits to employees, should you have any. Some financial institutions offer a package of medical, dental, life and disability insurance at reduced rates for group purchase. Premiums are deducted from paycheques, and employees may sometimes opt out if they wish.

Personal Life Insurance

You may not be able to outsmart death, but there are ways to lessen the blow to the family you have left behind. If you have dependents, try to imagine what would happen to them if you were to die. Your family could be in dire financial straits within months or even weeks if you haven't foreseen how they'll replace the lost income. And what about ongoing payments? The mortgage on the house? Daycare costs while your spouse works? Plans for your children's education? All these are at risk if you don't have enough life insurance. What is life insurance intended to do?

- It provides your beneficiaries with replacement income (some expenses, such as the cost of daycare, a housekeeper, and home repairs may increase).
- It creates an estate to carry through your goals for the future (support and education of children, future allocations for spouse, charitable causes, etc.).
- It protects the assets you've acquired so that they won't have to be

WHAT DO YOU NEED?

Singles

If you are single and without dependants or significant debt, you probably don't need life insurance. Your money may be better invested in a regular savings program. You probably want to ensure that you have enough money to cover such depressing expenses as a funeral and burial plot should you die. If you have sizable debts, you might consider buying term insurance (see below).

Families

If you still have a young family, you are in the greatest need of protection. Life insurance equal to at least 10 times your income is a good starting point. A $300,000 life insurance policy would provide an income of about $33,825 a year for 15 years (assuming an annual interest rate of 8 percent).

Don't overlook the need for life insurance for a stay-at-home parent. High-quality childcare and domestic help can be very expensive.

WHAT'S YOUR TYPE?

No matter what kind of insurance you buy, the premiums will be based on four factors:

- age
- health and smoking status
- coverage amount
- length of coverage

Ask your financial advisor to help you do a proper needs analysis. Factor in all of your current expenses, plus the replacement of the lost income and saving for retirement. Remember to allow for inflation.

sold to pay outstanding debts, such as a mortgage or the capital gains taxes accrued on your investments.
- It covers death expenses and debts.

Term insurance

A term plan provides protection for a set length of time — usually one, five, ten, or twenty years. Should you die during that period, your term policy will pay a specified amount to the beneficiaries you name.

Term insurance is the most affordable kind of life insurance, so it's a good buy for young families. You can usually renew your term when it's up. But though the premiums may seem pretty affordable in the beginning, they will increase with each policy renewal. As long as you pay the premiums, your insurance company can't deny you renewal because you've developed health problems. But most term policies do not allow you to renew after age 75 or 80, by which time the premiums would be very expensive. You usually have the option of converting the policy to one of the company's permanent insurance products without having to prove that you are in good health. But sometimes the costs of converting can be high if you wait too long. The earlier you convert, the lower the cost for permanent insurance will be.

Permanent insurance

This insurance covers you for as long as you live. It renews automatically for your entire lifetime, provided you continue to pay the premiums. The most common types of permanent insurance are whole life and universal life.

Whole life

Whole life insurance offers a guaranteed amount of insurance coverage for life, as well as a cash value fund that keeps the premium costs level. Premiums are fixed and guaranteed for a set number of years or for life. However, whole life policies are more expensive than term policies.

The cash value is a tax-deferred savings fund. But it makes the policy more expensive. If you want to borrow the cash value, you have to pay interest on the loan, and the death benefits will be reduced unless the loan is paid back. The growth in the cash value can give you additional options, such as extended coverage or lower premium payments.

Universal life

Universal life also provides insurance coverage for life, combining a self-directed savings portfolio with the insurance. The difference is that in whole life the cash value fund is invested as the insurance company sees fit, whereas in universal life you get a say in how it is invested. Any gains on the withdrawals you make from the savings portion are taxed and the plan could be subject to surrender charges if you cash it in. If you borrow against the policy, that amount may be charged interest and the proceeds will be reduced unless the loan is paid back.

Disability Insurance

It's easy to feel invincible when you are young and healthy. But, chances are you or someone close to you may become disabled at some point. If you are ill, injured, or permanently disabled, where will your income come from?

The government

You're probably well aware that government insurance isn't generous. So it's never wise to rely solely on government support. The Canada/Quebec Disability Pension Plan applies to those who have contributed to the plan for a minimum of two to five years if the disability is "severe and prolonged." The pension is made up of two parts: a flat-rate amount and an amount based on how much and for how long you paid into the CPP/QPP. But the total is minimal. As well, you'll likely have to wait between 12 and 24 months to receive your benefits.

Private disability insurance

You can qualify for 60 percent of your current income on certain conditions, and the benefits are tax-free. Watch for plans that pay back some of your money if you don't make a claim. The premiums are more expensive, but if you are in good health, they may be worth your while. When shopping for a private disability plan, ask these questions:

- Can I afford the premiums? If not, what alternatives do I have?
- What is the definition of "disabled"?
- What circumstances are excluded from the plan?
- How long is the waiting period before benefits are paid out?

- How long will the benefits be paid?
- What happens to premium payments while I'm disabled?
- Is there inflation protection?
- If I don't claim insurance, will I get any money back?

Critical Illness Insurance

This type of policy pays out a sum of money if you contract a specified illness, such as cancer or Multiple Sclerosis. You can use the proceeds to pay for treatment, to subsidize your income, take a vacation, or for whatever purpose you want.

Summary: Looking Out for the Future

As long as you have assessed your needs correctly, you should be able to find insurance that will protect and provide for you in the case of expected and unexpected eventualities. Remember to shop around, and resist anything unnecessary. Over time, make sure your policies reflect your changing needs.

QUICK RECAP

1. **Insure yourself for your sake, your family's, and your business's.**

2. **There are lots of kinds of insurance available — get the policies that suit your needs.**

3. **Make sure that the personal insurance coverage you choose complements the coverage you have through your business. Are there overlaps or gaps?**

CHAPTER 6

A Taxing Subject

Tax Strategies for the Small Businessperson

There are, essentially, three types of small businesses, and each has its own tax advantages and pitfalls. The way you structure your business determines not only your costs, but also the extent of liability for your business debts, the amount of growth possible, and the complexity or simplicity of your tax returns. The sector of the economy you choose to enter — whether it's retail, service, or manufacturing — and the projected initial size of your enterprise influence the structure. The main types of small businesses are sole proprietorships, partnerships, and corporations. These types have subtypes such as commercial or private partnerships, and some businesses, including franchises, appear not to fit any category, but here is an overview of the main three.

Sole proprietorships

A sole proprietorship can be anything from a consultant who hangs out a shingle, to an extended family running a huge eatery that is owned by one of the family members. The essence of the sole proprietorship is that, in the eyes of the government (whose eyes matter most when it comes to taxes), it is a private, unincorporated company owned by a single person. This person is in direct control of the business and is therefore responsible for all aspects of the business. One down side to having your own little kingdom, however, is that it can be hard to raise money. Unincorporated businesses tend to appear fairly unstable to those with money to invest, and usually debt financing is the only sure way to raise capital. And when you own a sole-proprietor business, every asset from wedding rings to weed whackers can be seized from the owner in payment of the business' debts. The official term for this is "unlimited liability."

Some owners of sole proprietorships attempt to circumvent unlimited liability by signing away all of their assets to members of their family. Before doing that, however, be aware that those assets will now be subject to the creditors of your family. Also, there are legal implications to transferring assets when the creditors are on your doorstep.

Businesses with little start-up capital requirement or with a labour-intensive product or service are the best candidates for sole proprietorships. Most freelancers and small service providers, such as jewellers and artisans are sole proprietors.

Partnerships

Partnership businesses are not limited to the traditional ones formed by doctors, lawyers, and hairdressers. For example, many restaurants and bars start off as partnerships between an administrator and a chef, as do such diverse enterprises as convenience stores, dance studios, and even some small factories. Often, a sole proprietorship will grow into a partnership as more capital or varied skills are needed. However, many entrepreneurs shy away from sharing decision-making authority with several others in a business, as it is sometimes difficult to find partners with both ability and money.

Partners are both jointly and individually liable for all of the debts of the business. Although partners can invest in a way that allows limited liability, for legal reasons such limited partners cannot participate in decision making. Partnerships, dependent as they are on the participation of two or more people, are also subject to the upheavals of death, illness, changes of heart, and midlife crises.

Limited partnerships are becoming a popular way to raise capital from "silent" partners while passing on the tax shelter of start-up losses.

Corporations

A corporation is an entity created by law that can own assets and incur liabilities. Incorporating a business offers several advantages, one of which is limited liability for all shareholders. Although they cost more to start up, corporations also boast transferable ownership, because they exist as legal entities, separately from their founders. Provincial law may prohibit certain professionals from being incorporated.

Corporations also have a few tax benefits. Although good bookkeeping is essential to any small business, the controlling and regulating bodies are especially strict about this for corporations. Preparing the large amount of paperwork the government requires can take a lot of time and money.

QUICK STATS: THREE TYPES OF SMALL BUSINESSES

Proprietorship

definition: owned by one person

common types: small retail, professionals, consultants, freelancers

advantages: owner control, no complicated legalities

disadvantages: unlimited liability for owner

Partnership

definition: owned by more than one person

common types: professional practices, smaller businesses of any kind

advantages: access to more people's capital, opportunity to combine skills

disadvantages: need for agreement among partners to make major decisions, joint and several liability, whole business affected by changes in personal lives of any of the partners

Corporation

definition: has legal status separate from owners, owned by one or more shareholders

advantages: limited liability for all shareholders

disadvantages: stringent regulations

To incorporate or not to incorporate

The decision to become a corporation — that is, a separate legal entity from the people involved with the business — is frequently (although, not always) based on the profitability of the business and the risk involved. Gord and Sally are book lovers and businesspeople at the same time. They employ six people in their store and they have a regular payroll. They also pay insurance on their store and their inventory and do some advertising in the local papers.

Should they incorporate? Yes. With a workforce of six and all those books on consignment, they wouldn't want to make themselves personally liable for the company's debts should bad times befall it.

HIRE JUNIOR!

There are considerable benefits to be had from hiring family members or spouses. As a small business owner, you might be in the 40 percent tax bracket, but your husband might be in the 25 percent bracket. If you pay him to work in the business, not only does more of that money stay in the family, but you can deduct the cost of that labour from your business. So you win both ways. Be careful though: this legitimate tax strategy has been used as a dodge. If you're paying your daughter $10,000 a year to turn the light on every morning before she goes off to her real job, you won't get a tax deduction. The employment should be real, and the remuneration realistic.

TRANSFER INVESTMENT INCOME TO YOUR CHILDREN

You can also split your taxable income with your children to lower your bill. Attribution rules limit income splitting with children under 18, but this doesn't apply to capital gains, income earned on income, or paying your child a reasonable salary for work performed in the family business.

BUSINESS STRUCTURE: WHICH IS BEST FOR YOU?

Type of Business	Advantages	Disadvantages
Sole proprietorship:	• Single tax return	• Sales of business could involve disclosure of personal tax returns
	• Losses deductible against other personal income	• Full liability for business debts
		• Highly profitable business is taxed at the highest personal rates (usually higher than corporate rates)
Partnership:	• Partners can deduct losses against other personal income	• Each partner is fully liable for all partnership debts (except limited partner)
		• Additional tax return is required if there are more than 5 partners
Corporation:	• Many tax reduction strategies available including small business rates, capital gains exemptions	• Much more complicated tax structure and filing procedures
	• Ease of transferring business	• Directors of company could still be liable
	• Liability limited to investment	• Tax losses remain with the corporate entity, not available to shareholders

Preparing Your Personal Taxes

Taxes are inevitable. They're also subject to constantly changing laws, they're complex and annoying, and it's hard to know how to maximize your savings. Whether you're a corporation with 50 employees, or you own a luggage store with your brother, here are some ways to (almost) breeze through tax time.

1. File all relevant documents throughout the year, including T4s, T5s, charitable tax receipts, T4RSPs, and the Notice of Assessment the government sent you after you filed last year. (It contains such useful tidbits as your RRSP limit for the current tax year.)
2. The law states you are required to keep all documents pertaining to your income tax for six years from the date of filing.

    Since no accordion folder can stretch that much, here's an idea: after you've filed your tax return, put slips, receipts, etc. into suitably marked envelopes. Put all these in a drawer in your filing cabinet. Keep this information in the back of your filing cabinet for six years, and you'll never have reason to fear an audit. Certain permanent business records must be kept beyond the six-year limit.
3. Find an accountant. As a small business owner, an accountant is an essential (and deductible) expense. Good accountants can probably save you untold grief and money if they're familiar with your line of work, since the tax department's rules are complex and ever-changing. Ask people in your field to recommend someone.

Salary? Dividend? Owner's Draw?

There are different ways for your company to pay you. You can receive a salary, much like other employees, or you can borrow from the company (this is called an owner's draw) and repay it at the end of the year by declaring either a bonus or a dividend. This explanation is grossly simplified. You should have your accountant or financial advisor look closely at your tax situation and your company's tax situation, and arrange for your payment to be in the form that will attract the least total tax. Other factors to consider are the effect on your RRSP contribution limit and your ability to get loans (loans officers look warily at people applying for loans whose tax returns show zero income).

SAVVY TAX TIPS

1. Use an RRSP to reduce your tax burden. Every penny (to a maximum of your contribution limit) is deductible and is also completely tax-sheltered as long as it stays in the plan.

2. If necessary, borrow to reach your maximum RRSP contribution. The long-term benefits of the RRSP generally far outweigh the loan interest. You might even find yourself with a refund, which will help to pay down the loan.

3. Use spousal RRSPs to reduce your own tax burden later in life. A lower-income spouse will also pay lower taxes on the redeemed funds in the future.

4. Consider income splitting. Reduce your household tax bill by using the higher-income spouse's funds to pay for household expenses, while the lower-income earner uses his or her money for investments (the income from which will be taxed at a lower rate).

5. Hire your spouse. His or her salary will be taxed at your spouse's rate, and the business will be able to use the payments as a deduction.

6. If your business has to be split up because of a divorce, transferred holdings can either be valued at original cost or according to market value. At cost means no tax applies. But if the recipient spouse sells the asset before the divorce is finalized, the contributing spouse is left to foot the tax bill, since you were still technically married when they were sold. After the divorce, the recipient spouse foots the bill.

7. Hire your children in your business if they can provide a legitimate service. They can use the salary to pay for the extras that you would have had to pay out of your after-tax dollars.

8. Consider a registered education savings plan. Invest in your children's education and at the same time, shelter the earnings on the plan. (Unfortunately, you can't deduct the contributions to a RESP.)

9. Capital gains are not taxed until you liquidate the assets that are earning them, so timing the sale of capital assets can reduce the tax you pay.

10. The interest on money you borrow to lend to your business can be tax deductible in certain circumstances.

11. If your business is in your home, you can deduct a variety of expenses from your income. The most common are a portion of you rent or mortgage interest, property insurance, and cleaning costs — but there are many others.

12. A corporation can choose its own year-end. Doing so can have considerable tax advantages for the owner, mostly through deferring taxes.

Taxing Investments

One of the predictable ironies of investing is that the better you do, the better the government does. Every gain you make through your investment dollar is taxed by the government, but different kinds of investment gains are taxed differently. Here's how it breaks down:

Interest

Interest income — for example, money you earn on debt instruments such as bonds and GICs — is fully taxed. That is, if your marginal tax rate (your "tax bracket") is 50 percent, and you earn $1,000 in interest, then you'll pay the government $500 of that in tax.

Dividends

Dividends from Canadian companies are taxed differently than income from other sources. A dividend is an amount paid by a corporation to shareholders as a form of profit-sharing, and since the corporation has already paid tax on that income, the government has devised a tax credit system to reduce double taxation. The dividend received is increased by 25 percent, but there is a combined federal and provincial tax credit of approximately 20 percent of the grossed-up dividend of a Canadian corporation. For example, consider what happens when someone in the 50 percent tax bracket gets a $1,000 dividend. The dividend is grossed up to $1,250, so the tax is 50 percent of that, or $625. But there is also a tax credit of $250, so the total tax paid is $625 minus $250, or $375.

Capital gains

A capital gain (or loss) is the difference between the buying price and the selling price of an investment. If you make a capital gain on an investment, three-quarters (75 percent) of the gain is taxable and is taxed at your marginal tax rate. Since a capital loss can offset a capital gain, get advice on timing if you are selling investments.

There are special considerations on the disposition of qualifying farm property and shares of small business corporations in certain circumstances. These are discussed in Chapter 11.

Other types of tax shelters

There are other, more exotic types of tax shelters, such as tax credits related to the film industry, that you are bound to hear about. Be cautious with these shelters and don't get involved unless you have received professional advice.

Make Your Instalments

If your business is not incorporated, you may need to make quarterly tax instalments. Failure to make these instalments has severe consequences. Set aside the amounts you need to pay on a regular basis.

Summary

Taxes are a reality that business owners and employees alike have to contend with. No one likes parting with hard-earned money, but since you have no choice, your best revenge is to minimize the amounts you have to pay and plan ahead to make sure the amounts you owe have been saved for. You may also find yourself in the position of having to change the type of business (from unincorporated to incorporated) if the change will result in a major tax saving.

QUICK RECAP

1. **Determine what structure is best for your company: a sole proprietorship, a partnership, or a corporation.**

2. **Take advantage of ways to save on your taxes.**

3. **Pay your taxes quarterly to avoid a large lump-sum payment once a year.**

Investing in High Gear

John, our digital-design expert, knows a lot about other small, specialized companies in his field, and he has a hobby of investing in them. He does this as much to help the other companies grow as to help his own finances grow, and he thinks these investments will be sure winners because his own company has taken off so well. That's where John's got it wrong. Even though he has made some money from some of these investments, he has lost a lot more and doesn't even realize that he is far from breaking even. That's because small start-ups are one of the riskiest kinds of investment there is. Just because John has made a success of his company doesn't mean that these other new high-tech companies will. What John needs to do is talk with his financial advisor about how to diversify his portfolio so that it includes high-, medium-, and low-risk investments. He'll probably continue to dabble in these small-cap stocks, but as long as he has some blue-chip security to balance them out, he will have improved his financial health.

Once you've learned how to strike the balance between investing in your business and investing in your future, the next step is to develop investment habits. Since you already know the value of a dollar, you probably also know what's happening to your money as it languishes in a bank account. That's right: it's losing value to inflation. Only the wisely invested dollar grows in value as compared to inflation, and if you want your money to grow the same way your business does, you'll have to put it somewhere where it will work hard on your behalf.

Investing your money in the right place can give you financial security, increase your net worth, and take you many steps toward financial independence. You can set a sound investment strategy by understanding the characteristics of different types of investments and creating the right mix that helps your money grow and lets you sleep at night. As we pointed out in Chapter 1, your best way of developing that strategy is with the help of a professional financial advisor. Once you've found that person, and you're confident that they know how to approach your specific needs (and remember not every advisor knows the ins and outs of small business), then you need to define who you are and what you want.

Selecting a Financial Advisor

Financial advisors take the time to know the lifestyles and financial needs of their clients. They have invested their time and energy into becoming knowledgeable in investments, taxation, estate planning, insurance, and retirement planning. In addition, they may work with a network of specialists who can provide the in-depth knowledge needed to deal with situations as they arise. Search for a financial advisor who combines an understanding of people with knowledge of technical planning matters, and who is able to monitor the financial, economic, political, and social environments. Most will provide you with an opportunity to learn about the processes they use and will give you detailed information on the services they offer and the company they work for before expecting you to begin the financial planning process. Things to look for in choosing an advisor:

- You feel compatible with the advisor and feel you can work well together.
- The advisor has an appropriate educational background.
- The advisor belongs to a professional association that has a code of ethics and standards.
- The advisor works for an established, solid financial institution.

- The advisor is willing to explain how he or she comes to a complete understanding of your personal, family, and financial situation.
- The same advisor who meets with you initially will continue to work on all of your subsequent needs.
- The advisor will review your situation at least annually.
- The advisor fully reveals how he or she is compensated for working on your account.

Know Yourself

When you start setting up your portfolio, you'll have to do some soul searching to match your investment mix to your goals and time frame. Ask yourself first about your time horizon and risk tolerance. What is the worst-case scenario? Remember, it is always a good idea to have a professional advisor help you through this process. Take stock of who and where you are, where you want to go, and how long you have to get there. Find out what sort of risk you are comfortable with.

- **Attitude**: Are you the kind of person who lies awake worrying about whether your financial institution will be struck by lightning? If so, you probably won't tolerate a lot of risk in your investment portfolio, and you'd be better off investing your money conservatively.
- **Age**: How old are you? If you're young and have few responsibilities, you can afford to take greater risks and you have more time to ride out any market lows your investments encounter. Once you get older and closer to retirement, you'll want to shift some of your investments into a more conservative portfolio.
- **Responsibilities**: Who or what depends on your income? If you have dependents, a mortgage, or a substantial loan, you probably can't afford to take great risk, so you'll want to invest most of your money conservatively.
- **Cash flow**: What's your income like? If your cash flow is erratic or likely to decrease, you don't want to risk investing in something that is too volatile.
- **Net worth**: If you have a large cushion to soften the blow of any losses, a long timeline, and a growing tolerance for risk, you can afford to accept more volatility.

- **Time horizon**: The longer you expect to keep your money in an investment, the greater the volatility you can manage, because, over time, short-term drops in the value of an investment should be replaced by gains.
- **Desired rate of return**: Different assets have different risk levels and therefore different potential rates of return.

Assessing Your Risk Tolerance

Only you know your attitude toward risk, so you must assess your own comfort zone. Ask yourself, "What's the worst that can happen if this doesn't work?" If "the worst" is something you can live with, then the risk is acceptable. Keep in mind that there is risk in not investing or in investing where after-tax returns are less than inflation. The risk is that your purchasing power will decrease. Smart investing means having the right balance of different investments to provide long-term growth with a risk level that is acceptable to you. The longer you have until you need the money, the more you can use investments with higher variability. This is because historically markets have tended to climb over time while experiencing peaks and valleys. The mix and balance of your investment portfolio will evolve as you get closer to the time you need the money.

In determining what risk is acceptable to you, keep in mind your short- and long-term goals. If you are planning to buy a second home next year, you don't want to put your down payment money into the stock market now, no matter how high it's soaring. A market downturn that coincides with your purchase date would have a serious impact on your short-term goal.

Although assessing your risk tolerance is largely a personal matter, some principles apply to just about everyone. For example, a 40-year-old can tolerate more investment risk than a 60-year-old who is expecting to retire in the next few years. The closer you are to needing your nest egg, the less you're going to want to have in more volatile investments. One very rough way of calculating this "age/risk ratio" is to subtract your age from 100. The number left over will be the percentage that you can afford to put in higher-return, higher-risk investments, such as equities. So if you're 45, 55 percent of your investment portfolio might be in equities. As you get older, this percentage will shrink. An advisor can help you make the right decision on your investment portfolio mix.

WHAT'S YOUR TOLERANCE?

Risk means different things to different people. Here is a relative yardstick for investment risk that can help you decide where your emotional comfort level is.

None: Your only concern is for the security of your original principal and you aren't interested in retaining its purchasing power over time.

Low: You could tolerate a fluctuation of no more than 10 percent in the value of your investment, occurring rarely, and even this would make you uneasy.

Moderate: You would not panic over a fluctuation of 10 to 20 percent in the value of your investment at any given time, knowing that over the long term you would eventually benefit from a positive return.

High: You could handle a fluctuation of 20 to 50 percent in the value of your investment at any given time in return for the potential for longer-term growth.

Very High: You could tolerate a fluctuation of 50 percent or more in the value of your investment, as long as you'd see a large potential return in the future.

Managing Risk

You can't and shouldn't avoid risk, but you can manage it. It is rather like driving a car on a highway. There's always some risk of accident or injury, but you can "manage" the risk by wearing a seatbelt, driving at a sensible speed, ensuring that the car is well maintained, and so on. You can reduce the risk even further by not making the trip, or by never leaving your home. But in reducing the risk of a highway accident by never leaving your home, you increase the risk of business failure. Similarly, you can reduce the risk of investment losses to near zero by keeping your money under your mattress, but that increases the risk of losing purchasing power to inflation.

You shouldn't fret unduly about investment risk. The key is to understand the risks and, with the help of a professional advisor, build a portfolio that has the right level and mix of risks. You should, however, be aware of the different kinds of risk and how they affect different investments.

Inflation risk: This is a special concern for guaranteed investment certificates (GICs) and other so-called risk-free investments. If for example, inflation is 3 percent, a GIC at 5 percent will give a real return of only

2 percent over five years and you likely will have lost purchasing power after tax. Unless they are held in an RRSP, you must also pay tax on GIC interest annually.

Interest rate risk: As interest rates rise, the market value of bonds falls. This is a concern if you have to sell a bond before it matures.

Currency risk: Fluctuating exchange rates can cut into your return on investments made in foreign markets.

Economic risk: Certain industries are very sensitive to fluctuations in the economy. The auto industry tends to do well in good times. Others, including utilities such as electrical power and telecommunications, are less sensitive to economic cycles.

Industry risk: With the rapid pace of technological change, some industries such as the computer industry, are inherently volatile.

Company risk: When you own a stock, you own part of a business, and even businesses in booming industries can be poorly managed.

Credit risk: If you're buying bonds, you're lending money to a company or government. Interest payments could be suspended or you may not be repaid your principal if the borrower runs into financial difficulty.

Liquidity risk: How easy is it to get your money with minimal capital loss? An account at a financial institution is liquid. Real estate is less liquid because you can't sell it until you find a buyer.

Political risk: Governments change the rules.

Evaluating the Performance of Your Investments

The press have a lot to say about the performance of investments, particularly mutual funds. Sensational headlines with this week's tragedies and tomorrow's predictions abound. When evaluating your investments — either over your morning newspaper and coffee, or formally with your financial advisor — be sure to follow these three simple rules:

Compare apples to apples. A mutual fund containing Pacific Rim stocks is much more volatile than one containing mortgages. They are different asset classes, with different risks and serving different purposes in your investment plan. As you can see from the table on the next page, the best and worst one-year periods for these investments vary widely.

There are no crystal balls. No one could have predicted what day you should have invested in order to have "ridden the wave" to the one-year 129.5% return on Japanese stocks. If that sort of prediction were possible, everyone would also have avoided the single-year loss of −42.1% in the same market! Your best bet is to be in a mix of asset classes, all of the time. That's why mutual funds make such excellent sense for most investors and why it's so important to include foreign content in your long-term RRSP.

Time reduces risk. The one-year highs and lows in the table on page 75 demonstrate the relative volatility of each asset class. The average five-year returns demonstrate how time invested in a particular market or asset class reduced that level of volatility. Be patient if you can.

Developing an Investment Strategy

A sound investment strategy starts with a good understanding of your financial goals. One approach is to divide your assets into three "pots" — to meet short-, mid- and long-term goals. An example of a long-term goal is to create an investment portfolio that will provide you with the funds you need to retire comfortably in 15 years. A mid-term goal is to replace your car in five years. A short-term goal is to fund the down payment on a vacation property next summer. Assume only as much risk as you need to meet each goal.

Money from each "pot" can be distributed among three classes of investments: cash or cash equivalents, meaning liquid investments, such as government savings bonds, T-bills, and money market funds; fixed-income securities, which pay a fixed income and are held for a term of over a year, such as GICs, and fixed-income mutual funds; and equity investments, which can potentially provide the highest gains, but which also come with the greatest volatility, including Canadian and international stocks, and equity mutual funds. Think of your portfolio as being made up of both your RRSPs and your other investments, which are probably not tax-sheltered. In your short-term pot, you will want to have most of your investments in fixed income and cash equivalents. In your long-term pot, you should include more variable investments, such as Canadian and foreign equities, to achieve bigger rewards. The medium-term pot will contain a balance of the two.

CASH & CASH EQUIVALENTS

	HIGHEST 1-YEAR RETURN	LOWEST 1-YEAR RETURN	AVERAGE 5-YEAR ANNUAL RETURN
Savings Accounts	11.6%	0.5%	5.3%
90-day deposits	14.0%	4.5%	9.1%
Canada Savings Bonds	19.1%	5.1%	9.4%
5-year GICs	14.8%	5.8%	10.0%

FIXED INCOME INVESTMENTS

	HIGHEST 1-YEAR RETURN	LOWEST 1-YEAR RETURN	AVERAGE 5-YEAR ANNUAL RETURN
Mortgages	34.8%	−2.0%	11.7%
Bonds	55.6%	−10.4%	13.7%
Dividend Stocks	79.5%	−14.5%	12.5%
Real Estate	19.3%	−7.1%	7.5%

EQUITY INVESTMENTS

	HIGHEST 1-YEAR RETURN	LOWEST 1-YEAR RETURN	AVERAGE 5-YEAR ANNUAL RETURN
Canadian Index	86.9%	−18.5%	9.7%
U.S. Index	56.9%	−22.8%	15.7%
Japanese Index	129.5%	−42.1%	15.6%
World Index	63.5%	−23.2%	13.0%
European Index	111.5%	−23.5%	17.1%

INFLATION

	HIGHEST 1-YEAR RATE	LOWEST 1-YEAR RATE	AVERAGE 5-YEAR ANNUAL RATE
Consumer Price Index	8.3%	−0.2%	3.7%

Notes: This table contains historical data and there is no assurance that future results will be consistent with this table. All rates of return occurred during the period January 1, 1982 to December 31, 1996.

Asset Allocation

To tailor your portfolio to your own investment needs, ask yourself the following:

- How much do I need to keep available for emergencies and short-term goals?
- How much do I need to invest for the long term?
- Will I benefit more from a compounding rate of return or do I need income from my investments?
- What are the tax consequences of my investment?
- How much variability am I willing to take?

Your investment strategy should consist of dividing your assets in such a way that your investments are diversified. This strategy is called asset allocation. The strategy involves building a portfolio that consists of assets from each of the three asset categories (cash, fixed income, and equity), and, in each category, from both the Canadian market and international markets. How much you invest in each category is determined by your tolerance for risk and your time horizon. Peaks in the performance of one category will tend to balance out valleys in another, and the overall result should be closer to steady growth than you would achieve by putting all your eggs in one basket. Most financial professionals agree that asset allocation — the correct proportion of stocks, bonds and cash — is more important to total portfolio performance than picking the top performers.

If you suddenly wake up in a cold sweat on your fiftieth birthday and you realize that you haven't saved enough to maintain your lifestyle in retirement, don't panic and throw all your money into high-return, high-risk investments in the hope of making up for lost time. Without setting out a good strategy, you could end up losing more than you make. Make achieving a balance between risk and reward your highest priority, and you'll make the most of what you have.

As Markets Move — Stay the Course

Once you've developed your asset mix, review it at least annually and rebalance it to maintain your desired asset mix. Remember, you are looking for long-term growth, so don't vary your asset mix with every move in the markets. With retirement approaching, you can adjust your mix toward fixed-income securities and cash, maintaining a smaller percentage in growth investments. Remember that age may not be the most critical factor. The key is time, not timing. Don't tinker too often, and use an investment professional to help you build the right mix of investments.

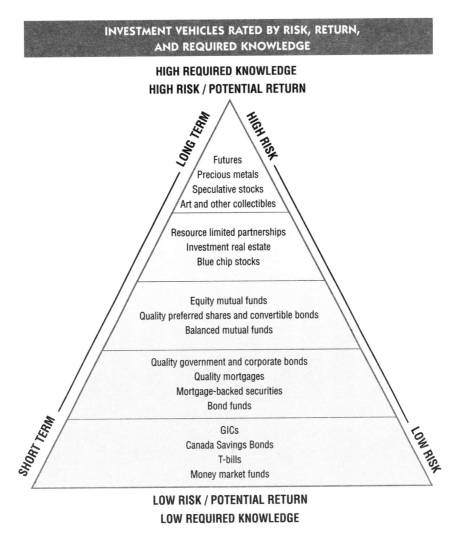

INVESTMENT VEHICLES RATED BY RISK, RETURN, AND REQUIRED KNOWLEDGE

HIGH REQUIRED KNOWLEDGE
HIGH RISK / POTENTIAL RETURN

LONG TERM

HIGH RISK

Futures
Precious metals
Speculative stocks
Art and other collectibles

Resource limited partnerships
Investment real estate
Blue chip stocks

Equity mutual funds
Quality preferred shares and convertible bonds
Balanced mutual funds

Quality government and corporate bonds
Quality mortgages
Mortgage-backed securities
Bond funds

GICs
Canada Savings Bonds
T-bills
Money market funds

SHORT TERM

LOW RISK

LOW RISK / POTENTIAL RETURN
LOW REQUIRED KNOWLEDGE

Dollar-Cost Averaging

Dollar-cost averaging is a technique that involves buying equal dollar amounts of a given investment on a regular basis, such as $100 every month. It works well for investments that fluctuate in price, such as shares and mutual funds. In fact, it lets you take advantage of those fluctuations. By buying a fixed dollar amount of an investment every month, you buy more units of the security when the price is low and fewer units when the price is high. If the investment tends to rise in price over time, the end result is a reduction of the average price paid for the investment purchased as demonstrated in the following three graphs.

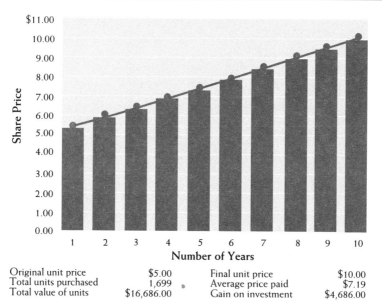

THE EVER-INCREASING PATTERN

Original unit price	$5.00	
Total units purchased	1,699	
Total value of units	$16,686.00	

Final unit price	$10.00
Average price paid	$7.19
Gain on investment	$4,686.00

THE DOWN-AND-UP PATTERN

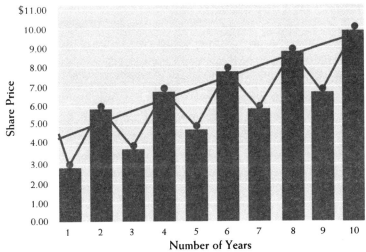

Original unit price	$5.00	Final unit price	$10.00
Total units purchased	2,075	Average price paid	$5.78
Total value of units	$20,746.00	Gain on investment	$8,746.00

THE DECLINE-AND-RETURN-TO-ORIGINAL-PRICE PATTERN

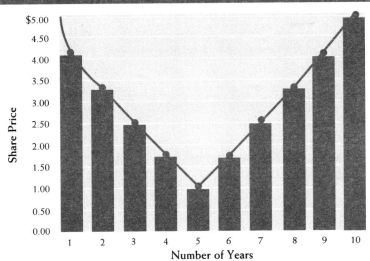

Original unit price	$5.00	Final unit price	$5.00
Total units purchased	4,829	Average price paid	$2.48
Total value of units	$24,147.00	Gain on investment	$12,147.00

Should You Pay Down Your Mortgage or Contribute to Your RRSP?

This is a question that a lot of homeowners ask because they often view both paying down their mortgage and building their RRSP as top priorities. The answer varies from person to person, and depends on factors such as your age and retirement plans. But ideally you should be able to do both. If you maximize your RRSP contribution, you can put your tax refund toward paying down your mortgage. Or, consider maximizing your RRSP this year and make a large mortgage payment next year. Don't forget that any unused RRSP contribution room can be carried forward to the next year.

Diversify Your Holdings

A successful asset mix depends, not on being in the right market at the right time, but on being in most markets all of the time, with varying exposures. If you've created an asset mix for your investments, you've already diversified your holdings to a degree. Diversification, however, doesn't just mean putting money into different investment vehicles. If you own a home, you have a substantial investment in your local community. If you're in a one-industry town, you work in that industry and have purchased stock in the company you work for, your assets are very concentrated. Look into investments that will move some of your assets out of your community, out of your industry, and even out of Canada — our economy can take a downturn while others are on the rise. International mutual funds now make these investments feasible, even if you're not among the jet set.

Summary

Your investment portfolio is a personal thing and should reflect you and your needs. The type of investments you should get into depends on factors such as your age, attitude, responsibilities, and when you want to retire. Working with a financial advisor is one way to feel secure about your investments. An advisor will help you learn about yourself by assessing what kind of investments are right for you, and will show you how to build a diversified investment portfolio that suits your needs. To get more out of your investments, use dollar-cost averaging and invest a fixed sum in your retirement portfolio every month. If you have planned your portfolio properly and feel confident in your choice of financial advisor, you should be able resist shuffling your investments around when periodic market scares strike. You and your professional advisor should review your portfolio at least once a year, but other than that, just sit tight and watch it grow.

QUICK RECAP

1. **Find a professional financial advisor with whom you feel comfortable.**

2. **Build your portfolio around your goals, risk tolerance, and time horizon, but remember that you can't avoid risk altogether.**

3. **Make sure that your total portfolio contains a mix of cash, fixed-income securities, and equity investments.**

4. **Review your portfolio at least annually, but don't react to every blip in the market — you are investing for the long term.**

CHAPTER 8

Investment Vehicles

Types of Investments

In order to be an informed investor, you should understand what you're buying, what the investment is intended to do, and what the risks and tax consequences of your investment are. Let's get started by looking at the two basic categories of investments: debt and equity.

Debt investments

Governments, corporations, individuals, and other entities borrow money for a variety of purposes. These loans are called bonds. If you invest in one of these, you are the lender. You want to know:

- your prospects for getting your money back,
- what income you can expect while you hold the investment, and
- when and how you will receive both.

Debt instruments pay you interest. Once a bond is issued, it gains in value if interest rates drop, and vice versa; therefore it may also provide capital gains or losses, which receive different tax treatment than interest.

Equity investments

These are usually shares in a company. They represent part ownership in the venture, with the prospect of all its risks and rewards. You need to know something about the company, its prospects, its market, and its competitors before you buy its shares. Equities offer the potential for capital gains and may pay dividends.

Variations on the basics

There is a wide variety of investment products. The best-known and easiest to understand are mutual funds. But whatever investment you choose, there is always more to know about it than first appears. It's essential to stay informed and up to date. Choose your advisors well.

Time and Timing

You can invest your money for periods ranging from less than 30 days to more than 30 years. Long-term debt instruments imply a forecast of inflation and interest rates for decades ahead — obviously something of a risk. If you're right, the rewards can be high. Some people still hold double-digit government bonds they bought when inflation was high. With stocks, the tendencies are reversed. They can be flipped in minutes, but that requires close attention and sometimes approaches gambling. Longer-term equity holdings are most consistently profitable. In general, short-term investing involves short-term management, which takes up more of your time — but any investment must be watched. It all boils down to when you buy the investment, how long you hold it, and when you sell it.

Value

When you're buying, selling, or trading investments, remember that the "value" of something — especially share equity — is not necessarily what you think it should be. It's no more than a buyer is willing to pay for it.

Looking into the Alternatives

What follows is a quick guide to the most common types of investments out there. They include debt and equity investments, and they have varying degrees of risk and reward. Read through these options and then talk them over with your financial advisor to decide which investments are right for you.

Types of Debt Investments

Interest or fixed-income investments

When you buy a fixed-income investment, your income is defined at the outset. It could be fixed or have different rates for different periods. You may receive your income when the term is up, or periodically over time. The same applies to your principal (if you invest in an amortized mortgage, for instance, with each payment you get some of your money back). If your risk tolerance is low, you'll want the majority of your investments in these vehicles. But don't expect to make your fortune this way. To calculate your real earnings, subtract taxes, then the rate of inflation. For example, suppose:

- your rate of return is 8 percent,
- you're in a 50 percent tax bracket, and
- inflation is 3 percent.

Your real rate of return is only 1 percent $(8 - 4 - 3 = 1)$. Your tax rate will be determined by your income bracket. Assuming your borrower is reliable, your two greatest risks in a fixed-income investment are that inflation will wipe out your earnings (suppose, in the example, that inflation hits 5 percent or 6 percent), or that you'll be locked into a fixed return when current interest rates rise.

Canada Savings Bonds (CSBs)

- these are specific government bonds that cannot be traded, only kept or cashed in
- pay interest (after the first three months) to the end of the previous month
- interest income is fully taxable each year when held outside of an RRSP
- a safe and easy investment
- available at most financial institutions

- set at a fixed interest rate (which may change over the course of the term)
- easy to cash (high liquidity)
- available for as little as $100

Treasury bills (T-bills)
- these government-issued investments pay a specified return for a specified (usually short) period
- interest income is fully taxable each year when held outside of an RRSP
- safe; considered equivalent to cash
- issued by the Government of Canada and provincial governments for terms of 91, 182, and 364 days
- can be bought and sold at any time from banks and brokers
- defined rate of return
- usually sold in amounts from $5,000 to $25,000 or higher
- bought at a discount and mature at face value

Term deposits
- vehicles for depositing a fixed sum of money for a fixed period of time at a fixed or variable interest rate
- offered by most financial institutions
- usually carry a guaranteed rate of interest for the length of the term
- interest income is fully taxable each year when held outside of an RRSP
- not meant to be redeemed, so if redeemed, may be subject to penalties
- $500 minimum, usually invested for periods ranging from 30 to 364 days
- may be covered by federal deposit insurance (CDIC)
- a term deposit of less than one year is called a certificate of deposit; anything longer is a GIC

Guaranteed investment certificates (GICs)
- interest-bearing deposits where interest can be paid periodically or upon maturity
- safe: covered by CDIC for up to $60,000 if purchased from an institution belonging to CDIC and the term is five years or less (If you have more than $60,000 to invest, buy from more than one insured institution.)

CDIC DEPOSIT INSURANCE

The Canada Deposit Insurance Corporation (CDIC) is a federal government agency that insures eligible deposits at member institutions. These include most banks and trust companies in Canada, but check if you're not sure whether a particular institution qualifies. If it does, your eligible deposits are automatically insured. "Eligible" means, generally, savings, GICs, chequing, and term deposits in Canadian dollars. GICs must be repayable within five years. The maximum amount the CDIC will protect in one name at one institution is $60,000 in principal and interest in all your deposits and accounts. If you have more to invest, spread it around among two or more institutions, depositing no more than $60,000 in each (allowing for interest). Using more than one branch of the same institution will not increase your coverage. However, there are other ways to increase your coverage: eligible joint deposits and RRSP deposits are insured separately. Each name or group of names is entitled to as much as $60,000 coverage for eligible deposits. Investments not eligible include debentures, foreign currency accounts, stocks, mutual funds, mortgages, treasury bills, and most bonds.

- interest income is fully taxable each year when held outside of an RRSP
- available at most financial institutions
- similar in structure and buying strategies to a term deposit
- cannot be traded; early redemption may be impossible or may involve penalties
- low minimums and limits, which are set by the institutions issuing them
- usual term is one to five years

Government bonds
- these bonds are a way of lending the government money for a fixed interest rate
- interest income is fully taxable each year when held outside of an RRSP

- a safe and easy investment
- available at most financial institutions
- set at a fixed interest rate
- can be traded, resulting in a taxable capital gain or loss

Corporate bonds

- these bonds are issued by a company and are a way of lending that company a fixed sum of money for a fixed amount of time at a fixed interest rate
- interest income is fully taxable each year when held outside of an RRSP
- can be safe or risky, depending on the company issuing the bond
- usually purchased through stock brokers
- usually easy to cash
- can be traded, resulting in a taxable capital gain or loss

Mortgages

- this type of investment lends money to a person or a pool of people to finance their homes, and is secured by the value of the property
- interest income is fully taxable each year when held outside of an RRSP
- safe or risky depending on the borrower
- have fixed or variable interest rates
- can be difficult to sell, however, a sale could trigger a taxable capital gain or loss

Strip bonds

(also called separately traded residual and interest payments, strip coupons, zero coupons, and term investment growth receipts)

- safer if government bonds rather than corporate bonds are involved
- bought at a "discounted" price, it yields the full amount at maturity
- deemed interest income is fully taxable each year when held outside of an RRSP (this is a complex topic — contact a financial advisor for more information)
- redeemable for a set amount at a future date (up to 30 years later)
- can be traded, resulting in a taxable capital gain or loss

Types of Equities

Common and preferred shares

Equity investments are more volatile than fixed income investments because the demand and supply for shares that determines their market value can be influenced by a number of factors. Share prices rise and fall with a company's earnings and prospects and the health of the market in general. Many factors are involved: rumours, government regulations, competition, and other developments that are impossible to predict. You hope to profit by selling the shares for more than you paid for them, creating a capital gain. You may also receive dividends — regular payments in cash or shares that give shareholders a piece of the company's profits. If the company has issued preferred shares, they may carry the bulk of the dividend, leaving little or none for common shareholders. The latter, however, get most of the benefit if the company's value rises.

Shares: (also called **stocks**) A share is a portion of the ownership of a company.

Bonds: A bond is a certificate that proves that you have lent a sum of money to a company or a government for a set amount of time at a fixed interest rate.

Common shares: Owning common shares in a company means that you actually own a part of that company. If the company's value on the stock market increases, you will make a profit; if it decreases, you will experience a loss.

Preferred shares: These shares pay a fixed dividend. If the company that issued the shares does poorly, the preferred shareholders are guaranteed to receive the dividend before common shareholders get anything. (If the company does *really* poorly, no one gets anything!) Conversely, if the company does really well, the preferred shareholder gets only the fixed dividend, and usually doesn't share in any "windfall" dividends.

Mutual funds: A mutual fund pools money from thousands of investors. The portfolio manager purchases a diverse portfolio of securities (stocks, bonds, and money market instruments, etc.) on behalf of the fund investors according to the fund's objectives. Diversification typically makes this kind of investment less risky than buying individual stocks.

Equities range from quite stable to wildly speculative, but even the safest can be more volatile than most fixed-income instruments. They can be very rewarding (in the long term, equities usually bring the greatest returns), but they can also make you nervous. At the nail-biting end are the penny stocks that rise and fall fast enough to take your breath away — and your money, too.

Remember that the more aggressively you play the stock market, the more hazardous it can be to your investments (and your sleep), especially in the short term. You should keep a cash cushion for emergencies. You need to know what you are doing. If you don't have time to manage your investments, find a financial advisor you trust who can help you build the right mix of investments. If you want to start investing but have little saved or don't have the knowledge to keep up to date, you're probably better off starting with a mutual fund.

Mutual Funds

Everyone knows about mutual funds, but not necessarily how they work. A fund pools money from thousands of investors to invest in a portfolio of securities on behalf of the investors, according to the fund's objectives. The securities can include one or more of the usual categories: stocks, bonds, real estate, money market instruments, or other investments.

This has several advantages. Diversification generally lowers your risk, but it's difficult to buy a variety of things if you don't have much money to invest. However, you can buy units in a mutual fund for as little as $500, and presto — it's diversified. The investment choices are made by full-time professional management teams with years of experience and

MUTUAL FUND POPULARITY

Everybody's doing it — your co-workers, your next-door neighbour, and maybe even your grandmother. But are your capital and rate of return guaranteed? No. Mutual funds are not protected by deposit insurance such as CDIC. You are protected if the mutual fund management company goes under since mutual fund assets are held in trust. The fund trustee would hire a new manager to administer the assets. But remember, there are no performance guarantees. If the value of the fund's holdings drops, the value of your investment drops.

SERVICE CHARGES AND FEES

1) Management Fees

- based on the value and growth of the fund
- about 0.5 to 3 percent of the asset value of the fund for the management and administration of the fund

2) No-load Funds

- units sold without any sales charge or commission fee; watch for higher management fees or hidden costs

3) Front-end Load Funds

- charge a percentage of your total investment at the time of investment, meaning that not all of the money you invest goes into the mutual fund. Generally not more than 5 percent

4) Rear/Back-end Load Funds

- commission is deducted when you redeem your investment — the longer you hold a mutual fund, the lower the redemption fee is. After a designated period, the back-end load usually disappears.

expertise who can thoroughly assess each investment in the portfolio. Fund managers often meet with the people who run the companies they invest in — something few individual investors could hope to do. Global markets can be difficult and risky for individuals; share prices of high-quality stocks may put them out of the reach of the small investor. However, mutual funds give you access to both. They're flexible as well: you can choose a variety of funds, as your needs dictate. Finally, mutual fund investments are not locked in, so you can generally redeem them at any time. The fund manager tracks all your transactions and provides regular statements and the information you need to file your annual income taxes. Of course, all those advantages come at a price. Managers charge a management fee to the fund for their services. In addition, you might pay a "load," or sales commission, to get into or out of many funds.

There are all sorts of mutual funds, offering very diverse investments. Here are a few of the common types.

Money market funds

- aim to provide income, liquidity, and safety of capital through investment in short-term money market vehicles (treasury bills, commercial paper of companies and government, etc.)
- return earned from interest paid on the investments
- low risk

Mortgage funds

- invest in residential and commercial mortgages
- achieve most return from income earned on mortgages and potential return from capital gains
- low risk in the case of residential mortgage funds, mortgage-backed securities, and commercial mortgages

Bond or income funds

- invest in the bonds of governments and privately held or publicly traded corporations
- return results from the interest income on bonds held and on potential capital gains
- low to medium risk, depending on type of issuing companies, governments, interest rate, economic environment, etc.

THE IMPORTANCE OF THE PROSPECTUS

A prospectus, in the investment world, is a document required by securities regulators for an offering of stock or other securities to the public. They're not easy reading, but they do contain important information about the issuer of the stock. For new companies you should consult a professional advisor. Mutual fund companies also issue a prospectus that states the fund's investment objectives, among other important details.

Dividend funds
- provide tax-advantaged dividend income with some possibility of capital growth
- invest in preferred and common shares
- medium risk

Balanced funds
- aim for some safety of principal and a balance between income and capital appreciation
- invest in a mix of stocks and bonds
- return realized from income earned from investments, as well as from capital gains
- medium risk

Equity funds
- medium to high risk, depending on type of stock
- aim to provide capital gains or appreciation
- invest in common shares
- prices can fluctuate in value more widely than other mutual funds
- return is the result of capital gains and income from its dividends

International and global funds
- medium to high risk, depending on objectives of the fund, currency fluctuations, geographic area, etc.
- seek opportunities in international markets that offer the best prospects for growth
- invest in one or more of bonds, equities, and money market assets

Sector (industry) funds
- seek capital gains and above-average returns
- invest in a particular sector or industry
- return results from growth in value of investments
- high risk — vulnerable to swings in the particular industry

Real estate funds
- seek long-term growth through capital appreciation and the reinvestment of income

- are less liquid than other types of funds
- may require investors to give advance notice of redemption
- subject to regular valuation, based on professional appraisals of the properties in the portfolio
- high risk in recent years as a result of the real estate market

Ethical funds

- consider the ethical implications of each investment (e.g., might not invest in companies that profit from alcohol, pornography, tobacco, or armaments or in companies not meeting environmental screens)
- medium to high risk

Labour-sponsored funds

- not mutual funds but venture capital funds, which must be invested in small businesses
- offer tax breaks to investors: the amount is different in each province
- may not be redeemable in the first five to seven years, or may face early redemption penalties, depending on provincial legislation
- redemption charges usually apply for a certain period
- high risk, liquidity poor
- governed by provincial legislation; the regulations are different in each province

Index funds

- medium to high risk
- aim is to provide capital gains
- invest in the shares of companies that are included in a particular stock market index in the same proportion (i.e., a Canadian index fund would invest in the companies that make up the Toronto Stock Exchange (TSE) 300 Composite Index; an American Index Fund would invest in the stocks that make up the Dow Jones Industrial Average)
- return is the result of capital gains and income from its dividends
- managed so that it always mirrors the exchange index

Summary

Investing in a diversified portfolio is a great way to build assets for a comfortable retirement, but don't forget that even the safest investments carry some risk. You should take advantage of more than one of the many investment vehicles available to you. And remember that investing is an active process: you have to play a part in understanding the various types of investments. Find a financial advisor who can help you build and maintain the right mix of investments over the long term.

QUICK RECAP

1. **All investments carry some risk.**
2. **Review what kinds of investments are suitable for you and your situation.**
3. **Monitor your investments.**

CHAPTER 9

Good Debt, Bad Debt

Managing Your Debt

A common rule followed by personal financial advisors is that your debt-to-income ratio, that is, your monthly debt divided by the amount of your net income, should not exceed 40 percent. Count as debt the monthly payments on your rent or mortgage, auto loans, and the minimum monthly balance on your credit cards. Count as income your monthly income after taxes and business expenses. To calculate the percentage, divide the debt figure by the income figure.

Debt load is different for small business, simply because it's possible to keep bad business debt from infecting your personal finances. But having protection isn't a good reason not to manage your debt intelligently, whether it is personal or business debt.

Good debt, bad debt

An example of good debt is a loan that you take out in order to buy an RRSP, to upgrade equipment, or to take a course to learn new technology. When you borrow to make an investment, the interest is tax-deductible if the loan proceeds are invested in a vehicle that generates income. This does not apply to loans taken out to make an RRSP contribution; the interest on these loans is not tax-deductible.

Bad debt is the kind that you incur without getting anything valuable in return. High-cost debt is also bad debt. Maxing out your credit cards to eat at expensive restaurants and bars, to buy countless CDs, or to pay your cell phone bill are all forms of bad debt. This kind of bad debt is double trouble because it also means you haven't budgeted properly and are living beyond your means.

Carrying a lot of long-term debt means paying a lot of interest charges. Sometimes the interest can add up to many times the amount of the original loan. So look into ways to pay down your debt before it becomes a mountain.

Paying off bad debt

Even if you have managed to acquire bad debt, there are sensible ways to manage it.

- Prioritize your debts by paying off non-deductible high-interest debt, such as credit card balances and auto loans, before low-interest debt, such as bank loans.
- See if you are eligible for a credit card with a lower rate of interest and transfer your high-interest balance to the new card. This is where your previous good credit rating will come in handy.
- Get rid of extra credit cards. After all, how many do you really need? Cut them up, then pay off what you owe! Too many cards invite temptation — if you reach your limit on one card, it is too easy to pull out another.
- Beware of any retailer credit cards. Retailers charge huge amounts of interest, usually about 28 percent, and they accept most major credit cards, anyway.
- Consolidate your debts by combining lots of smaller loans into one large one at a lower interest rate. However, be aware that though the interest rate may be lower, you could end up paying more. Because your required monthly payments are lower, it may take you longer to pay back the debt, which could cost you more in interest in the long run.
- Consider dipping into your savings account or CSBs to pay off high-interest debt. The after-tax interest you lose on the cash or the bonds can be much less than the money you gain by retiring your unpaid credit card balance.
- Start paying with cash or by debit card. This way, you will know exactly how much you can spend and you will get into the habit

of living within your means. Think of a debit card as a kind of plastic chequebook, and note all of your debit card purchases as if you were paying by cheque.

- Pay off your other, higher-interest loans before you pay off your mortgage. Tax-deductible debt should be paid off last.

Making Debt Work for You

It may sound strange, but debt can work for you. By handling debt responsibly, you will gain a good credit rating, which can help when you need to finance bigger goals, such as buying a house, a vacation property, or the Porsche you've always wanted.

To Buy or Not to Buy?

Big-ticket items call for different strategies that are specific to each purchase and unlike routine expense management. You can buy, rent, or lease. Each choice has consequences. To buy, you may need to borrow. Things you should consider before you decide to buy:

- depreciation
- rising maintenance costs
- inflation (good for the value of your house, but a problem if you're living on a fixed retirement income)
- cost-benefit: could you put that money to work in a better investment?

Leasing versus Buying

Rather than buy, you can lease. Leasing involves a small down payment and a clean break at the end. For a car, that's the way to go, right? Think twice. Leasing used to be sold, possibly oversold, on its tax benefits and its supposed financial superiority. For most people, the income tax break is now small, or nothing at all. Revenue Canada put car leasing on a fairly even basis with conventional financing in 1991, and in 1997 drastically reduced the dollar limit on car leases. Any sales tax advantage disappears if you want to own a vehicle at the end of the lease — and chances are you will. The same applies to the low asset value on which lease financing is based. That only applies if you end up with no asset. Think about what your retirement expenses will be. Do you really want to be spending money on a lease? Or would you be better off buying now, so you don't have to pay for it later? Above all, don't let leasing tempt you to live beyond your means. Other leasing advantages are questionable. The more extravagant claims, the ones that may linger in the back of your mind, were made when leasing companies kept their information close to the vest. Faced with disclosure legislation in British Columbia and other provinces, they became more open, and less aggressive in their claims. Interest rates may be lower than elsewhere, but don't count on it. Leasing software is now available to let you perform the same calculations the companies make and compare a prospective lease with other means of financing.

Leasing has one major advantage for business owners. When you lease, you can write off the acquisition costs on your company's books as you make the lease payments. When you buy, you are required to depreciate the asset according to capital cost allowance rules. For example, consider a $30,000 car that leases for $400 a month. If you purchase the car, you can write off 15 percent of the cost in the first year, so you have paid out $30,000 but can only write off $4,500 of it that year. If you lease the car, you can write off all of the $4,800 you've put out for lease payments.

Look Before You Lease

Leasing leaves you with nothing at the end except an option to buy. If you walk away, you've done yourself out of an asset. On top of that, there may be repair costs to bring a vehicle up to the leasing company's projected end-of-lease value, and a distance charge for too many kilometres driven. If you lease, your monthly payment is based on:

- the price of the item,
- the interest rate charged by the leasing company,
- the anticipated resale (residual) value of the item at the end of the lease,
- the length of the lease (usually two to four years), and
- the down payment you make (if any).

Here are some benefits to leasing:

- There is a minimal down payment, if any.
- Monthly payments are usually lower than if you purchased the item using a bank loan.

- It is easier to be approved for a lease than for a bank loan.
- There are cash flow advantages to leasing.

Leasing has its disadvantages, as well:

- At the end of the lease you have nothing to show for it — you haven't added to your assets.
- If you want low monthly payments you may have to make a down payment.
- To lower those payments you may have to accept a higher residual value at the end of the lease. You have to pay that amount if you want to buy the item. If you don't, you must hope that someone else will pay it. If not, you may be responsible for the shortfall.
- If the leasing company gets more than the residual value when it sells the returned asset, you will not benefit.

As you get closer to retiring, the disadvantages of leasing increasingly outweigh the benefits.

What Kind of Loan Do You Need?

Before you get a loan for a major purchase, you should consider the alternatives.

Fixed-rate versus variable-rate instalment loans

Two of the most common types of loans are fixed-rate instalment loans and variable-rate instalment loans. With a fixed-rate instalment loan, the term and the interest rate are set when you get the loan and they do not change. The monthly payments are a combination of the principal repayment and the interest, and because they never change, you always know how much to budget for. A variable-rate instalment loan differs from a fixed-rate instalment loan because it reflects fluctuating interest rates. A variable-rate loan is pegged at a specified percentage above the prime lending rate, and the interest that you pay will fluctuate with changes in the prime rate. You repay the same principal amount from month to month, but your interest will vary. With a variable-rate loan you will save money if interest rates decline, but it will take longer to pay back your loan if interest rates rise.

Demand loans

Demand loans are quite risky. With a demand loan, the lender usually sets a repayment schedule covering the term of the loan before lending the money, but the lender can also demand that the money be paid back in full at any time. This is known as "calling" a loan. The consequences for your finances can be very severe if your loan is called without advance warning. Financial institutions commonly offer small businesses demand loans, so beware.

Lines of credit

A personal line of credit is the most common and convenient type of variable-rate loan. Once you are approved for a line of credit, you can draw on it at any time, up to the pre-determined limit, with special cheques or a credit card. A normal line of credit starts at about $5,000, and many people find it convenient to pay for high-ticket items, such as home improvements, vacations, computer equipment, or investments, with a line of credit. The terms of repayment are set in advance, and the interest rates can be better than those on an unpaid credit card balance.

There are two different types of lines of credit: secured and unsecured. A secured line of credit, such as a second mortgage, offers collateral for the loan and usually has a lower interest rate. An unsecured line of credit is not backed by collateral and usually carries a higher interest rate.

Summary

Throughout your life, you will continue to use debt, through big purchases or simply through your regular monthly expenses. Nobody's life is completely debt-free. But there are right ways and wrong ways to accumulate debt. If you play your cards right and manage your debts, you can keep buying assets that increase your net worth (and are just plain enjoyable) and keep yourself comfortably in the black.

Good Debt, Bad Debt 101

QUICK RECAP

1. Pay off any bad debt you have.
2. Finance your purchases with the lowest-interest loans possible.
3. For most people, a secured line of credit is the lowest-interest-rate type of loan available.

CHAPTER 10

Family Financial Planning

Gord and Sally don't like the idea of making wills and deciding who will get what when they die. They never thought they had much to include in their wills anyway, until did their net worth assessment and took a good look at the numbers. And when Gord's brother recently had a heart attack (the same thing that killed his father and his uncle), they realized that it was high time that they made wills. Their children have made it clear that they don't want to run the bookstore in the event of their parents' death, but the whole family has never discussed future plans other than that. Even though they aren't looking forward to talking about death with each other and their children, they know that once they do, they'll all feel better about the future.

Have Your Circumstances Changed?

The last time you sat down and really thought about your circumstances and how they may have changed was probably when you tied the knot. Or when you pinned your first diaper. But a lot may have changed since then. You may have had more children, you may now be single, or remarried. You may be caring for your aging parents and start-ing to worry about whether your kids will do the same for you. You may be occupied with the thought of retiring, either on your own, or togeth-er with your spouse. Whether you have moved, inherited another prop-erty, lost that property to a divorce, or merged properties through a remarriage, your changes in assets and family responsibilities (read expenses) will have a dramatic effect on how you manage your finances. Although everyone's family situation is unique, this chapter will cover some of the more common changes people encounter, and show you some ways of dealing with those changes.

Yours or Ours?

Whether you have stayed married or have remarried, consider the financial implica-tions of your life as a couple. Are you both happy with the way you divide up expenses and assets, or is one of you shouldering too much of the burden? If you are paying alimony to a former spouse, you probably won't be able to afford half the expenses. But if your business has just taken off, it may be time for you to offer to pay more than half the expenses. Or if the busi-ness has hit a rough patch, you may want your partner to cover your half for a while.

MARRIAGE MEANS REASSESSMENT

If you're getting married, remarried, or starting to live together, you probably want to get things right. It is important to identify what you and your partner own, both jointly and separately. Here are some suggestions to make your joint financial life a success.

- Draft an upfront agreement (consult a lawyer if you feel you need to).
- Redraft your will.
- Be honest about any debts or financial responsibilities that you have. That includes alimony and child support you may have from previous marriages.
- Talk about what kind of lifestyle you both want (what's your definition of a luxury?)

CERTAINTIES OF LIFE

There are good reasons to name your spouse as your beneficiary when you contribute to an RRSP account. However, there could be other costs, so consult your advisor. When you die, your spouse can transfer the funds into his or her RRSP account on a tax-deferred basis. If you leave your RRSPs to your children, parents, or anyone else, the value of the RRSPs will likely be taxed in your name in the year that you die. This is not the case if you have no spouse and the money goes to a financially dependent child or grandchild. You should consult your lawyer about the implications to your estate plan of not naming a spouse as a beneficiary of an RRSP, RRIF, or life insurance policy.

The Financial Aftermath of Divorce

Since divorce is stressful both emotionally and financially, this is a good time to let a professional take some of the burden from you. Call a family lawyer, your financial advisor, and perhaps a tax advisor in addition to your friends and family. With proper support, you can make the process less painful. When dividing your assets from the marriage, get independent legal advice — don't rely on your ex's financial advisors to counsel you on what is your due. Assets could come to you in various forms:

- You may receive the family home.
- You may receive a lump-sum payment or other assets toward your settlement.
- You may be entitled to a share of the CPP/QPP or workplace pension that your spouse contributed to during the marriage.
- You might be able to share funds accumulated in your spouse's RRSP. The amount you are entitled to will depend on the family property laws of the province where you live. But you may be able to equalize your assets through a transfer: divorce is one of the few instances in which a transfer from one RRSP to another, owned by your spouse or ex-spouse, is allowed. Keep in mind that an RRSP carries a future tax liability (i.e., one dollar in an RRSP is worth somewhat less than one dollar in after-tax assets).

Spousal Support

Both men and women can apply for spousal support. Canada's Divorce Act sets out four objectives for spousal support:

- recognition of the economic advantages and disadvantages to spouses arising from the marriage breakdown,
- apportionment between the spouses of the financial costs of raising children,
- relief of financial hardship, and
- promotion of self-sufficiency.

The courts are more likely to order permanent support for spouses who had been homemakers during the marriage, but the level of support is usually quite low. Some courts do recognize that a homemaker's contributions (not necessarily financial) to a marriage can have lifelong effects on that spouse's earning potential.

Child Support

Federal and provincial governments have recently introduced measures to improve the level of child support and to make sure it is paid. The new regulations state that parents who fall too far behind in their payments could lose their passports. If evaders can't be found, Revenue Canada will open its data banks to help provincial enforcement agencies identify their employers and garnish their wages. Some provinces have more regulations than others, so find out your rights if you have a deadbeat ex. For agreements signed on or after May 1, 1997, child support is not taxable to the parent who receives it and is not deductible for the person who pays it.

PRIME-TIME EARNERS

When you do your yearly assessment, if you are divorced, make sure you include alimony and child support in your new budget. Think of this as protecting your children, rather than preparing for the worst.

Looking Ahead at Education

If you started a family late, you may be considering how to save for your child's education even as you're preparing to retire. You probably know people whose dreams of a university or college education were dashed because they didn't have the money to see it through. That's the kind of disappointment you don't want your children to face. Just as with your own retirement savings, you can take advantage of the power of compound returns. The money you put away every month will eventually grow enough to finance the high cost of education. A mere $100 invested monthly at 8 percent (compounded monthly) can grow to over $40,000 (before taxes) in 15 years. That should still be enough to pay the tuition fees for a typical undergraduate degree at a Canadian university, even if you allow for inflation and taxes.

Child tax benefits

If you receive a monthly child tax benefit, you could put it toward your child's education. Revenue Canada bases the amount and eligibility on your income, your child's age, and the number of children you have. If you deposit this payment into an account that is in your child's name, the income it earns will be taxed in the child's hands.

Registered Education Savings Plans (RESPs)

RESPs are a popular way to save for higher education. You have several types of plans to choose from, which will invest your money in numerous ways, including insured mortgages and deposits, depending on the terms of the plan. To set up an RESP, you make a contribution and name a beneficiary. Although your contributions are not tax-deductible, the earnings accumulate tax-free until they are withdrawn. When your child attends university, he or she becomes eligible to receive payments from the plan. Income from the plan is taxed in the child's hands. Capital can be returned to the contributor or paid to the beneficiary. In either case, a return of capital is tax-free.

In 1997, the federal government changed the legislation so that spouses may be joint subscribers, and if the designated beneficiary does not pursue post-secondary education by the age of 25, the earnings from a plan that you have had for 10 years can be moved into the contributor's RRSP, as long as the amount is not over the contributor's RRSP contribution limit. You also could take the earnings as income, but you will be taxed on them and will have to pay a 20 percent penalty.

Formal trusts for your children's education

As an alternative to an RESP, you might consider establishing trusts with formal written trust agreements to fund your children's education. This can have advantages for income splitting purposes but requires detailed tax planning and advice.

Caring for Aging Parents

Taking responsibility for your aging parents can be emotionally and financially draining, especially if you're still looking after your children's upbringing. Before it's too late, sit down with your siblings, your spouse, and your parents to talk about what kind of financial assistance or care they may need. Will they be able to afford it, or will they expect you to help out? Is that expense built into your savings, or will you have to mortgage your retirement to pay for theirs? Here are some suggested conversation starters:

- Who has power of attorney? (See the next chapter for more on the legal implications of a power of attorney.)
- In case of illness, who is the primary caregiver?
- Whose insurance will cover medical treatment?
- How much money do they need to save to pay for the kind of care they may need? Will the kids be expected to chip in? Too many children don't know enough about their parents finances when they start caring for them.
- Can they afford the kind of help they may need?

It's a delicate subject, and can raise a lot of sensitive issues. But not talking about it is bound to raise more problems and is just avoiding the inevitable. Knowing what your parents want before they need it will make decisions much easier for everyone in the family. We'll continue this discussion in a legal context in the next chapter.

Summary

A family is a micro-economy that needs to be managed well and wisely. When you started a business, you made a business plan. When planning your future, remember to take into consideration the different stages your family goes through as a whole.

QUICK RECAP

1. **Marriage (or divorce) means re-assessment: work out a financial plan that makes both partners happy.**

2. **Setting up ways to pay for your children's education will give them a head start on their own finances.**

3. **Be financially prepared for taking care of your aging parents or in-laws.**

CHAPTER 11

You Can't Take It with You

Death and Taxes

Why do we spend so little time planning for the certainties in life? Unless you want to be in trouble with the government, you have to keep your taxes in order. But preparing for the big event — death — is left entirely up to you.

Maybe you think that death is the last thing you need to worry about, since once you're gone, it's not your problem. But it will be your family's problem. By creating a solid estate plan, you will ensure that the people you care about are looked after when you're gone.

You'll also have peace of mind in knowing that your affairs will be looked after in accordance with your wishes. Estate planning ensures that what you leave behind goes where you want it. If it's done right, you'll be able to transfer and preserve your wealth in an effective and orderly manner. It also avoids needless taxation, delay, probate expenses, and family conflict.

Minimize, Minimize

To maximize the size of your estate for your heirs and to ensure your survivors are properly provided for, your goals are to:

- minimize the amount of taxes your heirs must pay on estate assets
- minimize the trauma and difficulties for your heirs, who need to organize your affairs when grief-stricken about their loss

Your Game Plan

- Determine how you want your estate to be distributed upon your death.
- Determine the amount of money required to provide for survivors and dependents, as well as funeral costs and probate fees.
- Consult with your financial advisor to determine if you need insurance.
- Have your lawyer prepare a will to distribute your estate assets.

What You Need in Order to Plan Your Estate

- financial plan
- will
- executor
- power of attorney
- guardian (if you still have minor children)

Estate Planning for the Small Businessperson

The fate of your business is a major part of your estate planning. Failing to make provision for what should happen to your business upon your death is a major oversight and can create undue stress for family as well as business associates. The type of business you're in will determine how you prepare.

Sole proprietorship

Unless you've made provision for a family member or an employee to take over or purchase your business, it will be liquidated upon your death. With a sole proprietorship, the business necessarily dies with the owner, but some assets may have value, such as client lists. It may be that this is your wish. Since business, personal assets, and liabilities are merged at death, business assets must be liquidated to settle the estate if debts need to be paid. Obviously, you want to avoid the trying circumstance of a forced liquidation. It's essential that your wishes be clear in your will, and the key to good planning is good communication. If you wish an employee or a relative to acquire the business assets, the mechanics and financing for this transition have to be well in place before your death.

Liquidation of your business may result in taxable capital gains and in the recapture of depreciation on any capital assets.

The proceeds from the sale of your business can be part of your legacy to your heirs. In that case, an executor must dispose of the business assets, and is authorized to sell the assets at public or private sale, to settle not only price but timing and method of payments, to evaluate the amount of collateral required, as well as to deal with family members to effect such a sale. A well-drawn-up will frees the executor from personal liability for whatever reasonable course of action is taken.

Partnership

A true partnership (not just people sharing office space) can result in some delicate negotiations upon the death of one of the partners. Once again, planning ahead is the key. Partnerships may end through sickness, retirement, or death, but it is almost always in the interest of the surviving partners to carry on the business. To dispose of a partner's interest in the business, a qualified buyer must be found, and frequently that buyer is the remaining partners. This is often effected through a "partnership agreement," backed by life insurance, and it is structured to provide an income to the family of the deceased. The purchase price must take into account the value on a number of intangibles, such as the goodwill represented by that partner's repeat customers and work left in progress, and is usually agreed upon in advance in the partnership agreement.

Sale of a partnership interest could result in a taxable capital gain.

Corporations

Shareholders of a corporation should consult with professional advisors regarding the possible need for a buy-sell agreement to purchase the shares of other shareholders upon death, as well as any possible tax implications for your personal estate if you were to die and have your shares be subject to a deemed disposition.

Special estate planning considerations for the business owner

Chapter 5 discussed the use of insurance to fund buy-sell agreements —
an important element in protecting your interests when more than one
key decision maker is involved in your business. Another issue relating
specifically to small business owners is the deemed disposition of capital
assets on death for their fair market value. This can result in significant
taxable capital gains as well as recapture of depreciation, becoming taxable on the final return for the deceased. This deemed disposition
applies in both of these situations:

- shares of an incorporated business
- capital property owned by the business owner if the business is
  not incorporated (An exception exists if the capital property is
  being transferred to your spouse on your death. Another exception applies to qualifying farm property, which, in certain cases,
  can be transferred on a rollover basis to the deceased's child,
  grandchild, or great-grandchild.)

In certain circumstances, a capital gains exemption would allow up to
$500,000 of the gain on the disposition of shares of a small business
corporation or qualifying farm property to be exempt from tax. The
rules governing whether the asset qualifies are complex, so talk to your
tax advisor about these rules.

Estate freeze

Your tax advisor can also tell you whether you should consider an estate
freeze. The objective of an estate freeze is to rearrange your holdings
so that future increases in the value of capital assets accrue to the benefit of your heirs — thereby locking in or freezing the value of your
interest for tax purposes. This complex procedure also requires professional tax advice.

Drafting a Will

A will is a legal document that sets out how you want your assets to be
distributed. The act of writing a will is like a spring cleaning that gives
you a chance to see what you actually own. It also names an executor
— the person or corporation (in cases where a trust company acts as the
executor) that will administer your estate, distribute your property, and
sell your business, if required. If you don't have a will, provincial law,

rather than your wishes, will determine the distribution of your assets and will stipulate that your business assets must be sold. And if you have no relatives, the government will get everything. The complexities involved in business law make it important that you have a lawyer help you draft your will. Owning a small business is considerably more involved than having some cash and a coin collection. The risk of doing it on your own is that your will could end up invalid or not properly specifying what you want to happen to your estate. Your will should include:

- the name of your executor and a description of his or her powers,
- a list of beneficiaries and specific bequests and legacies, and
- terms of any trusts to be established.

Review your will every year to keep it up-to-date with changes in your life. Nearly every big change, financial or personal, can change your will. For example, if you are divorced, do you really want your possessions to end up in your ex's hands? And if you are remarried, your new marriage will overrule any previous wills you might have. That means your new spouse could end up with the family cottage. What if your business expands or you take on a partner? Take a look at your will once a year to make sure it is still up-to-date.

WHO CAN HELP

Here are a few professionals you may want to involve in drafting your will.

- lawyer
- accountant
- financial advisor
- trust company (can work with your lawyer or recommend one)

Grant a Power of Attorney

If you ever become incapable of managing your own affairs, you will need someone to look after your best interests. This is the person to whom you grant power of attorney. If you don't appoint someone, someone will need to apply to a court to be given authority to manage your affairs.

The person you appoint has the power to act on your behalf in all financial affairs, to sign your legal documents, and, in some provinces, to make health care decisions for you. They should be trustworthy, competent, objective, and familiar with your financial affairs; so for most people, a spouse is the ideal candidate.

It's a good idea to specify that your power of attorney be an enduring power of attorney. This will allow the person you appoint to act on your behalf after you become mentally incompetent. An enduring power of attorney remains in effect until you die. At that time, control of your estate passes to the executor of your estate.

What Happens If You Don't Have a Will?

If you die without making a will, provincial law dictates how your assets will be distributed. In most provinces the majority of your assets go to your spouse, with your child or children receiving a percentage of your estate. However, in some provinces the deceased's assets are divided equally between the spouse and children.

Name a Guardian for Minor Children

Choosing a guardian to raise your children if you and your spouse die is a practical but difficult decision. After all, you're not just choosing an individual; you are choosing that individual's immediate family, as well. When trying to decide who might be a good guardian, think over these questions:

- Will this person be able to care for the children until they reach the age of 18 (at the very least)?
- Does this person share your values and goals for your children?
- Is this person willing to shoulder the responsibility?
- Does this person have a good relationship with your children?
- Are you comfortable with this person's immediate family?
- Do you need to set up a trust for your children through your will that will be funded through life insurance made payable to your estate?

HELPFUL HINT

To protect minors, your will can establish a trust for their legacies. If you're concerned about the free-spending habits of your heirs, you can set out a plan for paying their inheritance in instalments.

Setting Up a Testamentary Trust

Trusts are one way of dealing with your assets after you die. They come with income-tax opportunities and burdens, depending on your circumstances. You need a lawyer to help you with this. Your property is transferred into the testamentary trust on your death. It is managed by a "trustee," who is responsible for carrying out the terms of the trust. There are many ways to use trusts, to provide for both minor and adult heirs.

Select a trustee
To create a trust to take effect upon your death, the trust is included as a provision of your will. There are two kinds of trustees: corporate trustees, such as a trust company; or individual trustees, such as a family member, lawyer, or friend. The position of trustee comes with a lot of responsibility. Appointing a family member is one possibility. A corporate trustee is also an option.

Make an Estate Plan

Without a financial plan, you won't even know what will be left over for your beneficiaries. Here are the basic elements that your plan should have:

1. Determine the value of your estate. Look at the net-worth statement you prepared in Chapter 2. Your assets should include any lump-sum benefits from your company pension plan, CPP/QPP, and life insurance.

2. Anticipate your estate's liabilities:
   - **Funeral costs** (you can prepay them by putting the money in a trust where it can earn some interest)
   - **Executor or administrator fee** (3 to 5 percent of the estate value)
   - **Legal fees** (should be less than 2 percent of the estate value)

- **Probate fees** These are court fees that vary from province to province but are based on the value of the estate.
- **Trustee fees**
- **Taxes** Capital gains taxes don't apply to assets that are transferred to your surviving spouse, but everything else is deemed to be sold at the date of death. Three-quarters of the capital gain is taxable on your final tax return. The principal-residence exemption still applies, and special provisions are available for certain farm property and some shares of Canadian-controlled private corporations.

3. Subtract your costs from the value of your estate to determine what you will be leaving to your beneficiaries.

HELPFUL HINT

You can minimize your probate fees by removing assets from your estate, but there are certain risks to doing so. **Be sure to consult a professional advisor first!** There are two ways to do this: Register property or bank accounts jointly so that they automatically pass through to the survivor, although this means sharing ownership and control of the asset during your lifetime. Designate beneficiaries to your insurance, RRSPs, and RRIFs. Caution: there can be tax and other consequences associated with adding an individual as a joint owner of capital property, as well as designating that individual as beneficiary.

Summary

To ensure that your estate is distributed smoothly, you need to start preparing now. Once you've set up your plan, review it annually. Since you care about those you'll leave behind, manage your estate planning actively to ensure that your intentions become a reality.

ESTATE PLANNING CHECKLIST

✔ draft a will
✔ review it regularly
✔ update it according to your changing circumstances and seek professional advice when needed
✔ keep abreast of changes in legislation
✔ communicate with family and employees about what will happen to your business
✔ make a financial plan to protect your estate's assets

QUICK RECAP

1. **Review your estate plan regularly, and include your family and employees in your discussions about the future of your business.**

2. **Re-evaluate your will every three to five years.**

CHAPTER 12

Going for Gold

Get ready to enjoy the rest of your life. Now that you've read this far, you know that financial planning isn't half as frightening as you once thought. And that you can balance your business life with your personal life without jeopardizing your finances or your future. Congratulations! This knowledge puts you way ahead of many people who are too afraid to begin even thinking about life in retirement or life without their businesses. Until now, you may have got by without putting much planning into how to keep your household and your business running. But you want to do more than just get by: you want to be able to retire comfortably, with the freedom to do what you want, and in the knowledge that you've done the best you could do in business and at home. That doesn't mean you have to tighten your belt to the point that you can no longer breathe. It's just means taking a bit of time to take stock of where you are and where you want to go. Then you can start making the smart decisions to get there. Planning for your future should become part of your life, it shouldn't take over your life. The whole point of financial health is to follow a few sensible steps to become financially secure enough to live the way you want to.

Start by Helping Yourself

A trained financial advisor is best equipped to help you plan right. Take as much advice as you can. But the trick is to also rely on yourself, your instincts, and your desires. You know better than anyone else what you need and what you want. Others can help you plan, choose between investment options, and better understand available strategies, but they can't do it all. Your money and your welfare matter most to you, and you, ultimately, are the best caretaker of your future.

If you have a spouse or business partners, talk to them about what they see in their future and your future together. You may find your visions differ slightly, but it's better to find that out now than when they decide to pursue new careers and you're left winding down the store on your own. Once you both know what you want, go back and retrieve those scribblings when you listed your assets, liabilities, and your savings goals, and then take a look at what you can do to make your present and your future more worry-free. If your main problem is your RRSP or lack thereof, take a look at your budget and how you can start devoting more of it to your retirement savings. If your personal and business finances look like a bramble patch, start working on untangling them so they can both grow. Don't be afraid to ask for help, from friends and your financial advisor.

Get into a Routine

Forget the maxim, you can't teach an old dog new tricks. If you need to, you can change your ways beginning today. Just remember: start small, and the amount will grow big. Being financially healthy means making financial planning part of your routine. With a few simple steps to get you started, you will quickly find you're on your way to building your net worth and financial independence. Now that you've read this book, you can start taking action. You wouldn't expect to lose weight by sitting on a sofa watching Jane Fonda do aerobics for you; nor should you expect that good intentions without action will get your finances in order. Start today!

ONE MORE TIME

As we told you in Chapter 1, the key to sound financial management and a secure financial future is to assess your situation regularly. Just in case it's slipped your mind, here it is again:

At least once a year, assess your financial situation, as well as your long-term and short-term financial goals. Establish a realistic and comfortable plan to achieve those goals. Implement your plan, keeping in mind your risk tolerance and time horizon. Use a financial advisor the same way you would use a doctor — take advantage of their expertise to ensure your financial health.

It's easy. Think of it as your annual review. Don't forget to review the following:

- net worth
- budget
- will
- retirement goals
- investment portfolio
- insurance needs

General Summary

1. Make a list of what you want to do in your life. Don't settle for less. You can make your goals happen.
2. Do a self-assessment and organize or clean up your filing system.
3. Assess your net worth, including valuing your business.
4. Take care of your credit rating.
5. Manage your debt. Make a plan to get rid of your debt before you retire.
6. Don't buy any big assets without considering how they will affect your retirement plans.
7. Review your risk tolerance and adjust your investment portfolio accordingly.
8. Don't steal from Peter to pay Paul: keep your personal finances separate from your business.
9. Maximize your RRSP contributions to maximize your tax savings.

10. Seek professional advice to determine the best structure for your business: sole proprietorship, partnership, or incorporation.

11. Review your estate plan regularly, and include your family and employees in your discussions about the future of your business.

12. Protect your business by having a shareholder or partnership agreement and adequate life and disability insurance.

Index